Bertolt Brecht: Plays, Poetry, Prose

Edited by JOHN WILLETT *and* RALPH MANHEIM

The Collected Plays
Volume One Part Four

Brecht's Plays, Poetry and Prose
annotated and edited in hardback and paperback
by John Willett and Ralph Manheim

Collected Plays

Vol. 1 (*hardback only*)	Baal; Drums in the Night; In the Jungle of Cities; The Life of Edward II of England; A Respectable Wedding; The Beggar; Driving Out a Devil; Lux in Tenebris; The Catch
Vol. 1i	Baal (*paperback only*)
Vol. 1ii	A Respectable Wedding and other one-act plays (*paperback only*)
Vol. 1iii	Drums in the Night (*paperback only*)
Vol. 1iv	In the Jungle of Cities (*paperback only*)
Vol. 2i	Man equals Man; The Elephant Calf
Vol. 2ii	The Threepenny Opera
Vol. 2iii	The Rise and Fall of the City of Mahagonny; The Seven Deadly Sins
Vol. 3i	Saint Joan of the Stockyards
Vol. 3iii	The Baden-Baden Cantata; The Flight over the Ocean; He Who Said Yes; He Who Said No; The Decision
Vol. 4i	The Mother; The Exception and the Rule; The Horatii and the Curiatii
Vol. 4ii	Round Heads and Pointed Heads
Vol. 4iii	Señora Carrar's Rifles; Fear and Misery of the Third Reich
Vol. 5i	Life of Galileo
Vol. 5ii	Mother Courage and her Children
Vol. 5iii	The Trial of Lucullus; Dansen; What's the Price of Iron?
Vol. 6i	The Good Person of Szechwan
Vol. 6ii	The Resistible Rise of Arturo Ui
Vol. 6iii	Mr Puntila and his Man Matti
Vol. 7	The Visions of Simone Machard; Schweyk in the Second World War; The Caucasian Chalk Circle; The Duchess of Malfi
Vol. 8i	The Days of the Commune
Vol. 8ii	Turandot; Report from Herrnburg
Vol. 8iii	Downfall of the Egoist Johann Fatzer; The Life of Confucius; The Breadshop; The Salzburg Dance of Death

Poetry

Poems 1913–1956

Prose

Brecht on Theatre
Diaries 1920–1922
*Short Stories 1921–1946
*Selected Essays

* in preparation

The following plays are also available (in paperback only) in unannotated editions:

The Caucasian Chalk Circle; The Days of the Commune; The Good Person of Szechwan; The Life of Galileo; The Measures Taken and other Lehrstücke; The Messingkauf Dialogues; Mr Puntila and his Man Matti; The Mother; The Resistible Rise of Arturo Ui; Saint Joan of the Stockyards

Bertolt Brecht Collected Plays

Volume One Part Four

Edited by
John Willett
and Ralph Manheim

In the Jungle of Cities
Translated by Gerhard Nellhaus

Eyre Methuen · London

Introduction

In the Jungle of Cities is the third of four full-length plays (the others being *Baal, Drums in the Night* and *The Life of Edward II of England*) which Brecht wrote in Bavaria before moving to Berlin in the autumn of 1924. In spring 1918, when he began work on the first of them, he was just twenty and a new student at Munich university. Six and a half years later he was a recognized, if controversial writer and the winner of a major literary prize. The best directors and actors of the day were performing his plays; he had also written many poems and short stories and directed one remarkable production. He had just been on the staff of the Munich Kammerspiele, one of the most enterprising small theatres in Germany, where his first and so far most successful play had been performed. Now he was about to go as a 'dramaturg', or literary adviser, to Max Reinhardt's Deutsches Theater in Berlin, at that time one of the world's three or four leading theatres.

Born on 10 February 1898, Brecht had been brought up in Augsburg, about forty miles west of Munich. His father, a native of the Black Forest, was sales director of the Haindl paper works there; his mother died in May 1920. *Baal*, whose first version was finished by July 1918, reflects much of the imaginary world of himself and his group of Augsburg friends, as well as the taverns and physical surroundings of the old city. For a few months just before and after the armistice of November 1918 he served as a medical orderly in a local army hospital, but had returned to Munich by February 1919, the early days of the Bavarian Soviet, during which he dashed off the first version of *Drums in the Night*. There he showed both plays to Lion Feuchtwanger, the author of *Jew Süss*, who was then living in Munich and had recently met him for the first time. His own drama professor Artur Kutscher was always bitterly critical of his work, but Feuchtwanger was encouraging, so that he began to make contact with publishers and, at the end of the summer vacation, to write theatre criticisms for the Augsburg Socialist paper. Five one-act plays, *A Respectable Wedding, The Beggar, Driving out a Devil, Lux in Terebris* and *The Catch*, are also thought to have been mainly written that year, as well as a wealth of lost or unfinished works.

Baal was accepted by Feuchtwanger's own publisher Georg Müller, who had also published Wedekind's collected plays, but was withdrawn when already in proof for fear of the censorship. *Drums in the Night* was shown by Feuchtwanger to the Kammer-spiele 'dramaturg' Rudolf Frank, who at some point in the summer of 1920 accepted it for production. Neither publication nor production in fact materialized for another two years, but the encouragement to Brecht was obvious. He left the university in the summer of 1921 and in November set out to try his luck in Berlin, a much more important city from the theatrical point of view.

The expedition was less successful than he had hoped. Neither the Deutsches Theater nor the State Theatre under Leopold Jessner would make any promises, and although Brecht was asked to direct Arnolt Bronnen's play *Vatermord* for the experimental Junge Bühne, it ended disastrously with a walk-out of the actors. He himself was taken to hospital suffering from undernourishment, due no doubt in part to the galloping currency inflation. But at least he made many connections or friendships which were to be important for his work: notably Bronnen (with whom he began collaborating on film treatments and various joint theatrical projects), Herbert Ihering the critic of the *Berliner Börsen-Courier* (a lifelong supporter, whose paper was later to serve as a launching-platform for many of his ideas), and Moritz Seeler the organizer of the Junge Bühne (who was to produce *Life Story of the Man Baal* in 1926). By the time of his return to Augsburg at Easter he had also completed the first version of *In the Jungle*.

In Bavaria 1922 was a Brecht year. Soon after his return the Munich Residenztheater accepted *In the Jungle*, thanks to the recommendations of its artistic adviser Jacob Geis and of its new chief director Erich Engel, who had arrived a few months earlier from his native Hamburg. *Baal* was at last published (by Gustav Kiepenheuer of Potsdam), while 29 September saw the première of *Drums in the Night*. Clearly this was very different from later Brecht productions, for Otto Falckenberg, the head of the Kammer-spiele, staged it in expressionist style with angular poses and sets to match by his own staff designer Otto Reigbert. But Ihering came from Berlin to review it, and in the *Berliner Börsen-Courier* of 5 October he wrote that 'At 24 the writer Bert Brecht has changed Germany's literary complexion overnight. Bert Brecht has given our time a new tone, a new melody, a new vision.' Here too was 'a physical sense of chaos and decay':

Hence the unparallelled creative force of his language. It is a language you can feel on your tongue, in your gums, your ear, your spinal column.

Ihering was known to be the judge for that year's award of the Kleist Prize. This had been founded in 1911 by a group of Kleist enthusiasts to celebrate the centenary of the poet's death, and was intended for writers who had yet to establish themselves. Up to its abolition in 1932 it was probably the most significant literary award in Germany, having previously been given to the playwrights Sorge, Unruh, Hasenclever and Jahnn, while in 1923–5 it went to Musil, Barlach and Zuckmayer. On 13 November the *Berliner Börsen-Courier* announced that it had gone to Brecht, and not for *Drums in the Night* only but for all three of his completed plays. 'Brecht's linguistic power,' said Ihering's citation,

> is even more richly developed in *Baal* and *In the Jungle*. His language is vivid without being deliberately poetic, symbolical without being over literary. Brecht is a dramatist because his language is felt physically and in the round.

Because *Drums in the Night* was generally regarded as the prize-winning play it was widely performed all over Germany, notably in Berlin immediately before Christmas, when Falckenberg again directed it for the Deutsches Theater with a first-rate cast. Brecht always claimed that he had only written it to make money, and certainly it differs in several ways from his other works. Alone of those in this volume it seems to contain no anticipations of his later plays.

In Munich for two nights after the première it was followed by a midnight show called *The Red Grape* (*Die rote Zibebe*, a name at one time given to the tavern in Act 4, and also used of the moon which hangs so conspicuously over the action). This was described as an 'improvisation in two scenes by Bert Brecht and Karl Valentin', the latter being a famous Munich music-hall comedian. In the first scene Max Schreck, the actor who played Glubb, was the Freakshow Landlord who opened a series of curtained cabins, each containing a performer who stepped out to do a solo turn. The programme shows that these included the sailor-poet Joachim Ringelnatz, the reciter Ludwig Hardt, Brecht himself singing songs, and the dancer Valeska Gert, though for the second performance Brecht seems to have been replaced by his fellow-poet Klabund. The second scene was a sketch called 'Christmas Evening' by Valentin, whom a short programme note by Brecht compared with

Chaplin, among other things for his 'virtually complete rejection of mimicry and cheap psychology'. Valentin's influence has sometimes been seen in Brecht's farcical one-acters, though Brecht himself acknowledged it rather as affecting his work as a director, particularly his use of grouping.

That October Brecht was appointed to the Kammerspiele's dramaturgical and directing staff, where his main task was the adaptation and production of Marlowe's *Edward II*. The actual writing of this play, which is very largely an original work, must have taken place mainly in the winter of 1922–3, since the Berlin State Theatre started showing an interest in it early in the new year. It was done in collaboration with Feuchtwanger, whom Brecht saw frequently throughout 1923 and who is said to have inspired the speech characteristics of Shlink in *In the Jungle*. It was not however performed till the next year, and although there were two more Brecht premières in 1923, neither was at the Kammerspiele itself. First *In the Jungle* was staged at the Residenztheater on 9 May by Engel, with settings by Brecht's school-friend Caspar Neher: the beginning of a lifelong collaboration between the three men. Jessner of the State Theatre came from Berlin, as did Ihering, who again wrote enthusiastically, though not without observing that to anyone insensitive to its language the play must appear a muddle. This the local critics bore out; the three-hour performance was poorly received; it ran for only six evenings, and altogether was a disastrous enough flop to occasion the sacking of the theatre's artistic adviser. Nor was *Baal* in Leipzig at the end of the year any more successful. Alvin Kronacher's production at the Old Theatre on 8 December was taken off by order of the city council within a week, and the director reprimanded. It brought an interesting press controversy between Ihering and his rival Alfred Kerr as to the relative originality of Brecht and Toller, but Kerr was undoubtedly right when he wrote that 'The only hope for a Baalade like this is as a posthumous fragment . . .'. For the text as we have it was not performed again for another forty years.

The rehearsals for *Edward II* began that autumn under Brecht's own direction. Brecht also supplied the music; the sets were again by Neher, and as in the two previous Munich Brecht productions the actor Erwin Faber played the lead. The première on 19 March 1924 was somewhat thrown out by the drunkenness of one of the principal actors, but the local critics appreciated Brecht's success in conveying his ballad-like conception of the story (he apparently had the scene titles and dates announced before each episode), while Ihering was impressed by his handling of the ensemble scenes and the careful dissection of the long speeches. Knowing something of Brecht's as yet unformulated theoretical ideas, he realized that the audience with which he most sympathized was that for boxing matches, sporting events and incidents in the street, and attributed to this novel orientation part of the success of the production. Looking back two years later he saw it as something more: a major turning-point in the German theatre's understanding of the classics. For here had been an attempt at demonumentalization, an appeal for 'not so much plaster . . .' (the title of one of Brecht's subsequent essays), in which

> He did not analyse the characters; he set them at a distance . . .
> He called for a report on the events.

Viewed from 1926 it seemed like an early example of the 'epic' style.

Brecht's Munich period came to an end with the 1923–4 theatrical season, for once established in Berlin he remained based there until he went into exile in 1933. Only the one-acters had not been performed by the time of his move. *Baal, Drums in the Night* and *Edward* were all in print, while the *Hauspostille*, his first book of poems, was enjoying something of an underground reputation, having been announced as early as 1922, five years before its actual publication. That first winter in Berlin he was to have the rare distinction (for a young author) of two productions in the major theatres: *Edward II* directed by Jürgen Fehling (this gifted director's only Brecht production) at the State Theatre, with Werner Krauss as Mortimer and Faber once more as Edward, and *Jungle* at the Deutsches Theater directed by Engel, who had been lured to Berlin by Max Reinhardt a few months before Brecht. The outstanding young actor Fritz Kortner turned down a part in Reinhardt's *St Joan* in order to play Shlink: another indication of the interest already stimulated by Brecht's early work.

11

If the Bavarian years made Brecht's name they also established the main lines of argument for and against his work, with Kerr and Ihering respectively as counsel for the prosecution and the defence. Already the point at issue was his literary borrowings, and a number of later attacks on him (including that dealt with in the notes to *In the Jungle of Cities*) were foreshadowed in Kerr's *Baal* critique, with its dismissal of the play as second-hand Büchner and Grabbe. 'The gifted Brecht,' he wrote, 'is a frothing plagiarist.' To which Ihering countered:

> A writer's productivity can be seen in his relationship with old themes. In *Schweiger* Werfel invented a 'hitherto unheard of story' and was none the less imitative in every respect. Brecht was fired by Marlowe's *Edward II* and was creative through and through.

At the same time Brecht had been able to build the nucleus of his subsequent team of supporters and collaborators: first and foremost Neher, then Engel, the rather older Feuchtwanger, Kortner, Homolka, Klabund's actress wife Carola Neher and the playwright Marieluise Fleisser, all of them people who have left their individual marks on the German theatre. Here Brecht's personal magnetism clearly played a part: something to which there have been many tributes, starting with Feuchtwanger's fictional picture of him as the engineer Pröckl in his novel *Success* (1931). The first three plays all bore dedications: to his school-friend George Pfanzelt (the 'Orge' of the poems), to Bie Banholzer who bore his illegitimate son Frank (killed in the war) and to Marianne his first wife, whom he married in 1922. With *Edward II* this practice came to an end.

These were Brecht's pre-collectivist, indeed in a sense his pre-political years. He undoubtedly had opinions, many of them progressive and even revolutionary, but they were far from systematic, and politics and economics were wholly absent from what we know of his reading. On the other hand it was an extraordinarily tense and eventful time for Germany in general and Bavaria in particular, and Brecht was much too sensitive a writer not to reflect this in his work. A good deal has been made of his supposed pacifism in the First World War – though his schoolboy writings show that in fact he set out from a conventionally patriotic attitude and hardly developed beyond concern at the casualties – and of the impact made on him by his military service, which in fact was done on his own doorstep and in a hospital for venereal diseases, and started only a month or two before the end of the war. Several of the *Hauspostille* poems which are held to express his post-war sense of release had in fact already been written by then. Nor is there any evidence that he was more than a spectator of the revolutionary movements of November 1918, when the monarchy fell, and the first months of 1919, when Munich and Augsburg were governed by Soviets following Kurt Eisner's murder and the short-lived Spartacist revolt in Berlin.

Yet the 'Legend of the Dead Soldier' which he wrote in 1918 and took into *Drums in the Night* is always supposed to have earned him a place on the Munich Nazis' black list, while the play itself, though their paper the *Völkischer Beobachter* thought that it 'at any rate showed something of the idiocy of the November Revolution', struck none of the liberal critics as an unfair picture. It was certainly a very confused one, as the muddle over the dating of the action will confirm, and Brecht himself came to judge it in the severest terms, very nearly suppressing the play altogether. The revolutionary setting, however, was only a background to the real drama, and it had an instinctive poetic power which was not to be found in Brecht's later amendments.

The element of revolt in his writing of this time was largely directed against his own middle-class background: the satirical first scene of *Baal*, for instance, and the first two acts of *Drums in the Night*. Much of his reading, too, was exotic-escapist, as can be seen from the allusions in these plays to Gauguin and *Treasure Island* and Rudyard Kipling, and certainly this partly explains Brecht's interest in Rimbaud, whose elevated prose underlies Garga's 'psalmodizing' in *In the Jungle* (cf. Brecht's own semi-prose 'Psalms') and whose relationship with Verlaine was surely the model for that of Baal and Ekart. 'How boring Germany is!' says a note of 18 June 1920. 'It's a good average country, its pale colours and its surfaces are beautiful, but what inhabitants!' 'What's left?' he concluded: 'America!' That year he read two novels about Chicago, J. V. Jensen's *The Wheel* (which has never appeared in English) and Upton Sinclair's *The Jungle*, and when he began work on his own *In the Jungle* it was under their influence, intensified no doubt by his first experience of 'the crushing impact of cities' (about which he wrote an early poem) in the hard winter of 1921–2.

By the time of its first performance the French occupation of the Ruhr had given a great stimulus to nationalism throughout Germany, and not least to the Nazis in Bavaria. The *Völkischer Beobachter* particularly detested this play, claiming that the audience was full of Jews and that the Chinese characters spoke Yiddish. A month later Brecht and Bronnen heard Adolf Hitler addressing a meeting in a Munich circus, and were inspired (according to Bronnen) to work out what sort of a political show they could put on in a circus themselves. In November the Beer-Cellar Putsch interrupted the rehearsals of *Edward II* for a day. Brecht, with his colleague Bernhard Reich, went to call on Feuchtwanger, who saw this as the sign that they must leave Bavaria (and did in fact leave in 1924). But Reich recalls no particular concern with the Nazis on Brecht's part, and indeed not only was the putsch quite firmly suppressed – and Hitler jailed – but the stabilization of the currency by the Reich government set the Nazi movement back for a number of years.

The years 1918–1924 saw not only a certain element of political restoration throughout central and eastern Europe but also the end of Expressionism in the arts. To the poet-playwright Iwan Goll, who in 1921 published an essay called 'Expressionism is Dying', the two phenomena were connected. 'Expressionism was a fine, good, grand thing . . .' he wrote. 'But the result is, alas, and through no fault of the Expressionists, the German Republic of 1920.' Dadaism likewise was breaking up by 1922; at the Bauhaus the semi-mystical Itten was about to be succeeded by the technologically minded Moholy-Nagy; while artists like Grosz, Dix, Beckmann and Schlichter were evolving the coolly representational, socially conscious style which in 1924 became known as *Neue Sachlichkeit*. Brecht was always much too conscious of his own aims to care to be labelled as part of a movement; none the less his works of these years very clearly reflect the decline of Expressionism and the rise of the new style. He defined his position admirably in a note of 27 June 1920:

> I can compete with the ultra-modernists in hunting for new forms and experimenting with my feelings. But I keep realizing that the essence of art is simplicity, grandeur and sensitivity, and that the essence of its form is coolness.

Baal was written as a kind of counter-play to the Expressionists' invocations of Humanity with a capital H, yet the wandering poet remains a romantic-expressionist figure, while the influence of Georg Büchner is one that is also noticeable in a number of Expressionist plays. *Drums in the Night* too, with its symbolic use of the moon, its cinematic third act and its hero's slightly mad rhetoric, can reasonably be termed an Expressionist play. *In the Jungle*, however, was written at the turning-point, the watershed between the two movements. The Rimbaud allusions, the colour references before each scene in the 1922 version, the attic-cum-undergrowth setting, the use of spotlights referred to in Brecht's note of 1954: all this is expressionistic, whereas the American milieu, the preoccupation with the big cities and the very notion of the 'fight' were to become characteristic concerns of the mid-1920s. A further note of 10 February 1922 even suggests that Brecht was looking forward to his own 1930s doctrine of 'alienation':

> I hope in *Baal* and *Jungle* I've avoided one common artistic bloomer, that of trying to carry people away. Instinctively, I've kept my distance and ensured that the realization of my (poetical and philosophical) effects remains within bounds. The spectator's 'splendid isolation' is left intact; it is not *sua res quae agitur*; he is not fobbed off with an invitation to feel sympathetically, to fuse with the hero and seem significant and indestructible as he watches himself in two different versions. A higher type of interest can be got from making comparisons, from whatever is different, amazing, impossible to overlook.

Thus though *In the Jungle* is still wildly romantic it already foreshadows the detached impersonalities of the machine age. And those supporters who, like Ihering and Engel and Geis, thought that Brecht would help lead the theatre out of the Expressionist undergrowth can now be seen to have been absolutely right.

III

The final texts of these plays often make Brecht's evolution difficult to follow. He was a restless amender and modifier of his own work, so that any one of them may consist of layer upon layer of elements from different periods. 'He is more interested in the job than in the finished work,' wrote Feuchtwanger in an article of 1928 called 'Portrait of Brecht for the English',

> in the problem than in its solution, in the journey than in its goal. He rewrites his works an untold number of times, twenty or thirty times, with a new revision for every minor provincial production. He is not in the least interested in seeing a work completed. . . .

Thus between 1922 and its publication in 1927 *In the Jungle* became *In the Jungle of Cities*. The city allusions were strengthened, the boxing foreword was added and various boxing allusions worked into the text, the colour references at the start of each scene gave way to mock-precise ('objective') data of time and place, the whole flavour of the play was changed. The same was done still more drastically with *Baal* in 1926, though in this case Brecht later decided to scrap the more 'objective', technologically flavoured version and go back (more or less) to the 1922–3 text. *Drums in the Night* he seems to have left alone after 1922, perhaps because it was not performed again after the first, largely topical wave of interest had subsided. Then for his Collected Plays in the 1950s he largely rewrote the last two acts.

All this means that each play as we now have it reflects the views and to some extent the spirit of a number of different periods. The performances which have gone into theatrical history were not based on these particular texts. Even Brecht's own notes are difficult to understand without knowing to which version each of them relates.

It is an impossible problem editorially, and our policy has been to print the final text but to provide all the variant material from other versions published in Brecht's lifetime, together with extensive notes on the main unpublished scripts. This is so that the reader should not get false ideas of Brecht's evolution and of his ideas and achievements at any given time. Brecht was a profound believer in change, whom it would be wrong to present statically in a final 'authoritative' mould. Indeed opinions might well differ as to whether any such mould is the right one: not only are there fine things in many of the rejected versions, which it would be cruel not to publish, but informed judgement often disagrees with Brecht's last choices. Thus the chief German expert on *Baal* and the author of much the best book on Brecht's early years both prefer the 1919 script of *Baal*; an outstanding West German theatre critic wants the 1922 *Drums in the Night*; while Ihering wrote of the (final) published version of *In the Jungle of Cities* in 1927:

> I love the fullness and colour of the old *Jungle*. There seemed to be no better evidence of Brecht's richness and gifts than those crackling, exotically pulsating scenes as they shot to and fro. . . . The new *Jungle*, the *Jungle of Cities*, has lost in colour and atmosphere. It has gained in clarity and concentration.

Not that there is much chance that Brecht himself would have accepted his own choices as final if he had lived longer, or seen them staged, or looked again at some of the earlier texts which for one reason or another he did not have before him when preparing the collected plays. It is characteristic that he already wanted the 1926 version of *Baal* printed as an appendix. For he was always a man in motion, who progressed best by disagreeing with what had already been said. Often it had been said by himself.

The German text used throughout, unless otherwise stated, is that of the *Gesammelte Werke* (or Collected Works) edited by

Elisabeth Hauptmann and a team comprising Werner Hecht, Rosemarie Hill, Herta Ramthun and Klaus Völker, and published by Suhrkamp-Verlag, Frankfurt-am-Main, in 1967. This is referred to as GW, plus the appropriate subdivision: *Stücke* (plays), *Schriften zum Theater* (writings on the theatre), and so on. When the same terms (*Stücke*, for instance), are used without the prefix GW they refer to the earlier collected edition issued by the same publisher from 1953 on. Particulars of other sources are given in full where reference is made to them. We would like to thank the editors and publisher for the help which they have given with various queries. The Brecht Archive in East Berlin has been generous in supplying material, and we are grateful for the support given us from the outset by Stefan S. Brecht.

THE EDITORS

In the Jungle of Cities

*The fight between two men in the
great city of Chicago*

Translator: GERHARD NELLHAUS

Prologue

You are in Chicago in 1912. You are about to witness an inexplicable wrestling match between two men and observe the downfall of a family that has moved from the prairies to the jungle of the big city. Don't worry your heads about the motives for the fight, concentrate on the stakes. Judge impartially the technique of the contenders, and keep your eyes fixed on the finish.

Characters

Shlink the lumber dealer, a Malay · George Garga · John Garga, his father · Mae Garga, his mother · Mary Garga, his sister · Jane Larry, his girl friend · Skinny, a Chinese, Shlink's clerk · Collie Couch, known as Baboon, a pimp · J. Finnay, known as Worm, hotel owner · Pat Manky, a first mate · A Salvation Army preacher · Two Salvation Army girls · The pugnosed man · The barman · C. Maynes, owner of a lending library · Waiter · Railway workers

[Numbers in the text refer to notes on p. 84 ff.]

The Lending Library of C. Maynes in Chicago

The Morning of 8 August 1912
Garga behind the counter. The doorbell rings. Enter Shlink and Skinny.

SKINNY: If we read the sign right, this is a lending library. We'd like to borrow a book.

GARGA: What kind of a book?

SKINNY: A fat one.

GARGA: For yourself?

SKINNY *who looks at Shlink before each answer:* No, not for me; for this gentleman.

GARGA: Your name?

SKINNY: Shlink, lumber dealer, 6 Mulberry Street.

GARGA *taking down the name:* Five cents a week per book. Take your pick.

SKINNY: No, you choose one.

GARGA: This is a detective story, it's no good. Here's something better – a travel book.

SKINNY: Just like that you say the book is no good?

SHLINK *stepping up to him:* Is that your personal opinion? I'll buy your opinion. Is ten dollars enough?

GARGA: Take it as a gift.

SHLINK: You mean you've changed your opinion and now it's a good book?

GARGA: No.

SKINNY: Ten dollars will buy you some fresh linen.

GARGA: My job here is wrapping books, that's all.

SKINNY: It drives the customers away.

GARGA: What do you want of me? I don't know you. I've never seen you before.

SHLINK: I never heard of this book and it doesn't mean a thing to me. I'm offering you forty dollars for your opinion of it.

GARGA: I'll sell you the opinions of Mr J. V. Jensen and Mr Arthur Rimbaud, but I won't sell you my own opinion.

SHLINK: Your opinion is as worthless as theirs, but right now I want to buy it.

GARGA: I indulge in opinions.

SKINNY: Are your family millionaires?

GARGA: My family live on rotten fish.

SHLINK *obviously pleased:* A fighter! I'd have expected you to come across with the words that would give me pleasure and get your family something better than fish.

SKINNY: Forty bucks! That's a lot of linen for you and your family.

GARGA: I'm not a prostitute.

SHLINK *with humour:* I hardly think my fifty dollars would interfere with your inner life.

GARGA: Raising your offer is one more insult and you know it.

SHLINK *naïvely:* A man's got to know which is better, a pound of fish or an opinion. Or two pounds of fish or the opinion.

SKINNY: Dear sir, your stubbornness will get you into trouble.

GARGA: I'm going to have you thrown out.

SKINNY: Having opinions shows you don't know anything about life.

SHLINK: Miss Larry says you wanted to go to Tahiti!

GARGA: How do you know Jane Larry?

SHLINK: She's starving. She's not getting paid for the shirts she sews. You haven't been to see her in three weeks. *Garga drops a pile of books.*

SKINNY: Watch your step! You're only an employee.

GARGA: You're molesting me. But there's nothing I can do about it.

SHLINK: You're poor.

GARGA: I live on fish and rice. You know that as well as I do.

SHLINK: Sell!

SKINNY: Are you an oil king?

SHLINK: The people in your neighbourhood feel sorry for you.

GARGA: I can't shoot down the whole neighbourhood.

SHLINK: Your family that came from the prairies . . .

GARGA: Sleep three in a bed by a broken drainpipe. I smoke at night, it's the only way I can get to sleep. The windows are closed because Chicago is cold. Are you enjoying this?

SHLINK: Of course your sweetheart . . .

GARGA: Sews shirts for two dollars a piece. Net profit: twelve cents. I recommend her shirts. We spend Sundays together. A bottle of whisky costs us eighty cents, exactly eighty cents. Does this amuse you?

SHLINK: You're not coughing up your secret thoughts.

GARGA: No.

SHLINK: Nobody can live on twelve cents profit.

GARGA: Each man to his taste. Some people like Tahiti, if you don't mind.

SHLINK: You're well informed. That's the simple life. On Cape Hay there are storms. But farther south you've got the Tobacco Isles, and green rustling fields. You live like a lizard.

GARGA *looking out of the window, dryly:* 94 degrees in the shade. Noise from the Milwaukee Bridge. Traffic. A morning like every other morning.

SHLINK: But this morning is different; I'm starting my fight with you. I'm going to start by rocking the ground you stand on. *The bell rings, Maynes enters.* Your man has gone on strike.

MAYNES: Why aren't you taking care of these gentlemen, George?

SKINNY *bitingly:* His relations with us are strained.

MAYNES: What do you mean by that?

SKINNY: We don't care for his greasy shirt.

MAYNES: How dare you come to work like that, George? Is this a hash house? It won't happen again, gentlemen.

SKINNY: He's saying something. He's cursing up his sleeve! Speak up, man, use the voice God gave you!

GARGA: I must ask you for new shirts, Mr Maynes. You can't be a gigolo on five dollars a week.

SHLINK: Go to Tahiti. Nobody washes there.

GARGA: Thanks. Your concern is touching. I'll send my sister to pray for you in church.

SHLINK: Please do. She has nothing else to do anyhow. Manky's the right man for her. He runs himself ragged for her. Your parents are starving and she doesn't bat an eyelash.

GARGA: Are you running a detective agency? Your interest in us is flattering, I hope.

SHLINK: You're just shutting your eyes. Your family is headed for disaster. You're the only one who's making any money, and you indulge in opinions! When you could be on your way to Tahiti. *Shows him a sea chart that he has with him.*

GARGA: I've never seen you before in all my life.

SHLINK: There are two passenger lines.

GARGA: You just bought this map, didn't you? It's brand-new.

SKINNY: Think it over, the Pacific!

GARGA *to Maynes:* Please ask these gentlemen to leave. They didn't come to buy anything. They're driving the customers away. They've been spying on me. I don't even know them.

J. Finnay, called Worm, enters. Shlink and Skinny step back, pretending not to know him.

WORM: Is this C. Maynes's lending library?

MAYNES: In person.

WORM: Shady establishment, if you ask me.

MAYNES: Are you looking for books, magazines, stamps?

WORM: So there are books? Filthy business. What's the point of it? Aren't there enough lies? 'The sky was blue, the clouds flew east.' Why not south? What people won't swallow!

MAYNES: Let me wrap this book for you, sir.

SKINNY: Why not let him catch his breath? And I ask you, does this gentleman look like a bookworm?

GARGA: It's a plot.

WORM: You don't say! Listen to this. She says, 'When you kiss me I always see your beautiful teeth.' How can you see when you're kissing? But that's the way she is. Posterity will find out. The lewd bitch! *He grinds his heels on the books.*

MAYNES: Look here, sir, you've ruined those books, you'll have to pay for them.

WORM: Books! What good are they? Did libraries stop the San Francisco earthquake?

MAYNES: George, get a policeman.

WORM: I've got a liquor store. That's an honourable business.

GARGA: He isn't even drunk.

WORM: The sight of such loafers makes me tremble like a leaf.

GARGA: It's a put-up job. They're out to get me.
Couch, called Baboon,[1] *enters with Jane Larry. Worm steps back pretending not to know them.*

BABOON: Come on in, my little white chick. This is Maynes's rental library.

GARGA: You'd better close the shop, Mr Maynes. Strange vermin are crawling into your papers, moths are eating your magazines.

WORM: I always say: Look life straight in the eye.

BABOON: Get your face out of my way! I can't stand paper, especially newspaper.

GARGA: Get the gun!

SHLINK *steps forward:* I ask you again, will you sell?

GARGA *noticing Jane:* No!

JANE: George, is this your shop? Why are you staring at me? I was just going for a little walk with this gentleman.

GARGA: Keep walking.

BABOON: Say, let's not get rough. Don't you trust her? If I get excited, this book will end up in a thousand pieces. You still don't trust her?

MAYNES: I'll fire you if you won't trust her. My books are being ruined.

GARGA: Go home, Jane, please. You're drunk.

JANE: What's wrong with you, George? These gentlemen are being nice to me. *She drinks out of Baboon's bottle.* They've bought me drinks. It's hot today – 94. You know, George, it rips through you like lightning.

GARGA: Go on home now. I'll come tonight.

JANE: You haven't shown up for three weeks. I'm not going home any more. I'm fed up sitting around with those shirts.

BABOON *pulling Jane on to his lap:* That's all over now.

JANE: Oh, you're tickling me. Stop that! George doesn't like it.

BABOON: In brief, she's got a body that's worth a few bucks. Can you afford it, sir? It's a question of love and a question of drinks.

WORM: Maybe you'd like to keep her a virgin? What do you want her to do? Scrub floors? Wash clothes?

SKINNY: You expect a nice little pigeon like her to be an angel?

GARGA *to Shlink:* Are you trying to turn this place into the Wild West? Knives? Guns? Cocktails?

WORM: Hold on! You can't leave your job here. Maybe somebody will fall by the wayside. Sell!

GARGA: Strange. Everybody knows what's going on except me. – Jane!

BABOON: Tell him!

JANE: Don't look at me that way, George! This may be my only chance. Can you buy me drinks? Oh, it's not for the drinks! It's like this, George: every morning I look in the mirror. It's been two years now. You always go off and work for four weeks. When you were sick of it and needed liquor, you thought of me. I can't take it any more! The nights, George! That doesn't make me bad, not me. Don't look at me that way, it's not fair!

BABOON: That's smart. Have another drink and you'll be even smarter.

GARGA: Whisky's rotting your brain. Can you hear what I'm saying? Let's go away! Together! To Frisco! Anywhere you want. I don't know if a man can love for ever, but I can tell you this much: I'll stick by you.

JANE: You can't, Georgie.

GARGA: I can do anything. I can even make money if that's it. I've got a special feeling for you. There are no words for it! But we'll get together again. I'll come tonight. This very evening!

JANE: I hear every word; you don't need to shout and you don't need to tell these gentlemen here you didn't love me. You're only saying the bitterest things you know, and naturally I've got to listen. You know it as well as I do.

WORM: Cut the comedy! Just tell him you were in bed with this gentleman from nine to ten-thirty.

JANE: That might not be so good. But now at least you know, George, it's not the whisky or the heat!

SHLINK: Sell! I'll double the price again. This is so unpleasant.

GARGA: That doesn't count. What's nine to eleven against two years?

SHLINK: I assure you two hundred dollars means nothing to me. I hardly dare make such an offer.

GARGA: Would you be kind enough to send your friends away.

SHLINK: As you wish. Consider the ways of this planet and sell.

MAYNES: You're a fool and a dishrag and a lazy coolie; just think of . . .

SKINNY: Your innocent careworn parents!

WORM: Your sister!

BABOON: Your sweetheart! This lovely young girl.

GARGA: No, no, no!

SHLINK: Tahiti!

GARGA: I refuse.

MAYNES: You're fired!

SHLINK: Your economic existence! The ground you stand on! It's shaking!

GARGA: This is freedom! Here, take my coat! *Takes it off.*
Give it away! *Takes a book from the shelf and reads:* 'Idolatry!
Lies! Lechery! I'm a beast, a black. But I can be saved.
You're phony niggers, maniacs, savages, misers! Merchant,
you are a black and, Judge, you are a black, Emperor, you
old leper, you're a nigger, you drink untaxed liquor from
Satan's still. This people inspired by fever and cancer!'
Drinks. 'I'm unversed in metaphysics. I understand no laws.
I have no moral sense, I'm a brute; you are mistaken!'[2]
*Shlink, Skinny, Worm, and Baboon have gathered round Garga
and applaud as at a theatrical performance.*

SHLINK *smoking:* Why get so excited? Nobody's doing anything to you.

JANE *her arms round his neck:* Is it that bad, George?

GARGA: Here are my shoes! Are you smoking your little
black cigar, sir? It might make you dribble. Here, my
handkerchief. Yes, yes, I'll auction off this woman! I'm
throwing these papers in your face. I want the tobacco
fields of Virginia and a ticket to the Islands. I want, I want
my freedom. *He runs out in his trousers and shirt.*

SHLINK *calls after him:* My name's Shlink, Shlink the lumber-
dealer! Six Mulberry Street!

SKINNY: He'll toe the line . . . What's all this paper cost?

WORM: You're really going to pay?

MAYNES: The books are worth ten dollars.

SKINNY: Here's twenty.

BABOON *to Jane, who is crying:* Aha, now comes the awakening!
Go weep in the gutter.

WORM: You've got to look life straight in the eye.

SHLINK: How much is this stuff?

MAYNES: The clothes? Jacket? Tie? Shoes? They're not
really for sale. Ten dollars.

SKINNY: We finally drove him out of his skin. Let's take it
with us.
*Shlink goes out slowly towards the back, Skinny follows him with
the bundle of clothes.*

2

Chicago. The Office of C. Shlink, lumber dealer

22 August, shortly before 7 p.m.
Shlink at his little table.

SKINNY *voice from left rear:* Seven carloads of Kentucky.
WORM *in the rear:* Right.
SKINNY: Two carloads of stripped logs.
WORM: There's a man asking to see Mr Shlink.
SHLINK: Send him in.
WORM: Here's Mr Shlink!
  Garga enters.
SHLINK *please:* So here you are! Here are your clothes. Put
  them on.
GARGA: You've been waiting for me? You've brought my
  clothes here? Filthy rags. *Kicks the bundle of clothes away.*
  Shlink strikes a small gong.
MARY *enters:* George!
GARGA: You here, Mary?
MARY: Where've you been, George? They were worried
  about you. And the way you look!
GARGA: Just what are you doing here?
MARY: I take care of the linen. We can live on that. Why are
  you looking at me like that? You look as if you'd been
  having a hard time. I'm doing fine here. They said they'd
  fired you.
GARGA: Mary, pack your things and go home. *Pacing around.*
  I don't know what they want of me. They've harpooned me
  and pulled me in. I can feel the ropes. I'll have to depend on
  you, sir. But leave my sister out of it!
SHLINK: As you wish. *To Mary:* But first get him a clean
  shirt, and a suit. If you don't mind.
MARY: I can't understand my brother. He wants me to leave you.

SHLINK: And when you've finished, please go home too. I
don't know anything about linen.
Mary leaves.

SHLINK: Have you been drinking?

GARGA: Kindly tell me if that doesn't fit in with your plans.

SHLINK: I only have saki. But I'll get you anything you like.
You prefer cocktails?

GARGA: I do everything in one fell swoop. I'm in the habit
of doing nothing for weeks but drink, make love, and
smoke, all at the same time.

SHLINK: And leaf through the Britannica . . .

GARGA: You know everything.

SHLINK: When I heard about your habits, I thought to myself: There's a good fighter.

GARGA: What's the hold-up with those clothes?

SHLINK: Excuse me . . . *He stands up and strikes the little gong.*

MARY *enters:* Here's your linen, George, and your suit.

GARGA: Wait and we'll leave together. *He changes clothes behind
a screen.*

MARY: I have to say good-bye, Mr Shlink. I couldn't quite
finish the linen. Thanks for letting me stay at your house.

GARGA *from behind the screen:* This suit has no pockets.
Shlink whistles.

GARGA *coming out:* Who are you whistling for? In the last few
weeks you've got left, I want you to stop whistling for
people.

SHLINK: I accept your orders.

GARGA: You opened up this western. I'll accept the challenge. You skinned me alive for the fun of it. You won't
make amends by giving me a new skin. I'm going to wipe
you out. *Pulls a gun.* An eye for an eye, a tooth for a tooth.

SHLINK: Then the fight's on?

GARGA: Yes! Without obligation, of course.

SHLINK: And no question why?

GARGA: No question why. I don't want to know why you
need a fight. If you've got a reason, I'm sure it's rotten. For
me it's enough that you think you're the better man.

SHLINK: Well, let's think it over. Owning a house and a lumber business, for instance, puts me in a position to sick the dogs on you. Money is everything. Right? But my house is yours now, and so is the lumber business. From now on, Mr Garga, my fate's in your hands. I don't know you! From now on I'm going to be your slave. Every look that comes into your eyes will trouble me. Every one of your wishes, known or unknown, will find me willing. Your cares will be my cares, my strength will be yours. My feelings will be dedicated to you alone, and you will be an evil master.

GARGA: I accept your challenge. I hope you'll have nothing to laugh about.

Baboon, Skinny, and Worm enter silently. Garga notices with a grin that their suits are the same as his.

SHLINK: This house and this lumber business, carried on the Chicago Register of Deeds as the property of Shlink, are being transferred this day to Mr George Garga of Chicago.

GARGA *to Shlink:* That's me. All right. How many stripped logs have you in stock?

SHLINK: Maybe four hundred. I don't know exactly.

SKINNY: They belong to Broost and Company of Virginia.

GARGA: Who sold them?

WORM: I, known as Worm, owner of the Chinese Hotel in the coal district.

GARGA: Sell them again.

WORM: Sell them twice! That's fraud.

GARGA: Right.

WORM: And who'll be responsible for this order?

GARGA: Sell those logs in Frisco under the name of Shlink. Turn the money over to Mr Shlink, who'll hold it for me until I ask him for it. Any objections, Mr Shlink?

Shlink shakes his head.

WORM: That's barefaced fraud. We'll have the law on us in no time.

GARGA: How soon?

SHLINK: Six months at the most. *He brings Garga the ledger.*

BABOON: This is a bog.

GARGA: Storks thrive on bogs.

BABOON: It's better to work with a switchblade than with phony papers. Can you forget that Chicago is cold?

GARGA: You meant your actual lumber business, didn't you, Shlink? The house, the logs, the whole inventory?

SHLINK: Of course. Here's the ledger.

GARGA: Pour ink over the ledger. You!

SKINNY: Me?

Shlink hands him a bottle of ink.

SKINNY *over the ledger*: All these entries! All our transactions!

GARGA: Go ahead, pour!

Skinny pours carefully.

BABOON: That's that.

WORM: What an ending after twenty years! Some joke! I don't get it. This used to be a lumber business.

GARGA: And now turn off the saws and that will be the end of this lumber business.

BABOON: Anything you say, boss! *Goes out.*

The sound of the saws outside stops. Shlink's cronies put on their coats and stand against the wall. Garga laughs loudly.

MARY: What are you doing, George?

GARGA: Shut up! Fire that man, Mr Shlink!

SHLINK: You may leave.

SKINNY: Leave? After working in this place for twenty years come April?

SHLINK: You're fired.

MARY: I don't think you're doing right, George.

GARGA: I want you to go home, Mary.

MARY: And I want you to come with me. You'll only come to grief around here. Let him go, Mr Shlink.

SHLINK: Give me your orders, Garga.

GARGA: Certainly. As long as there's nothing left for you to do around here, my orders are to set up a little poker game with your former staff.

Shlink and his cronies sit down to play poker.

MARY: You're coming home with me, George. This whole thing is a joke, can't you see that?

GARGA: We grew up on the prairies, Mary. Here we're being sold out.

MARY: We? What do they want of us?

GARGA: You're of no consequence in all this. They're only trying to rope you in. Two weeks ago a man spat a small cherry pit into my eye. I come to see him. With a gun in my pocket. And he only bows and scrapes and offers me his lumber business. I don't understand a thing, but I accept. I'm alone on the prairie, and, Mary, I can't help you.

WORM *addressing Garga and Mary from behind:* He plays like a paper god. I swear he cheats.

GARGA *to Shlink:* I don't understand a thing, sir, I'm like a nigger in all this. I came with a white flag, but now I'm attacking. Give me the papers that are your fortune and hand over your personal assets. I'll put them in my pocket.

SHLINK: Paltry things, I beg you not to despise them.

Shlink and Garga go out.

SKINNY: Things were bad around here and the rain came in on us, but being fired is always an injustice.

WORM: Don't talk like a fool. *Mocking him.* He thinks we've been talking about the mildew in the floor.

SKINNY: I love you, lady. You have a way of holding out your hand . . .

WORM: Christ! He's lost his bed, and he wants a woman to share it.

SKINNY: Come with me. I'll work for you. Come with me.

BABOON *also comes forward:* Pitiful! There are all sorts of women, black and golden yellow and white like apples! Black women. Straight as a die from hip to foot! Full thighs, by God, not chicken legs like this! Oh Papua! Forty dollars for Papua!

SHLINK *appears in the doorway and turns to call offstage:* Yes, that's all.

WORM *to the Baboon:* You're a barbarian. Ungrateful! The lady's innocent. Does she smoke a pipe? She's inexperienced, but who's to say she has no fire? Forty dollars, and all for the lady.

SKINNY: As much as you want for her!

BABOON: Without make-up, naturally, uncooked, the naked flesh. Ah, the tropics! Seventy dollars for the chick!

MARY: Protect me, Mr Shlink.

SHLINK: I'm ready to protect you.

MARY: Do you think I should go with him?

SHLINK: Here nobody loves you. He loves you.

GARGA *has entered:* Do you like being for sale? There's a lot of lumber here, and now they've put a few pounds of flesh up for auction! And isn't jiu-jitsu known as the gay and easy art?

SHLINK *walks up to Garga, troubled:* But aren't you making things too easy for yourself?

MARY *to Garga:* You should have helped me. Come with me, George, this minute. Something terrible has happened. Even if I go away now, this thing may not be over. You must be blind not to see that you're losing.

In the background, the sound of two guitars and a drum. Salvation Army girls sing: 'Christ receiveth sinful men.'

GARGA: I can see you're ready to lose yourself. It's the bog that's sucking you in. Here's something for you, Mary. The Salvation Army! Marching in here for you. *He gets up from the table and goes to the rear.* Hey! Salvation Army! This way!

WORM *to Mary:* A river has drained off here, and at night the place is haunted by the ghosts of drowned rats. Go home to your parents!

GARGA *coming back:* Clean this joint up. Get rid of that whisky! *Shlink starts to do so, but Mary does it for him.* Come in, you people.

Shlink, bowing low, opens the wooden gate. A young Salvation Army preacher enters, followed by two girls with guitars and an old sinner with a drum.

PREACHER: Did you want me?

WORM: Hallelujah! The Salvation Army!

GARGA: I don't think much of what you people are doing. You could use a house though. Here, take this one.

PREACHER: The Lord will bless you.

GARGA: Maybe. *To Shlink:* Did you inherit this house and
these papers?

SHLINK: No.

GARGA: You worked forty years for them?

SHLINK: Worked my fingers to the bone. I never slept more
than four hours.

GARGA: Were you poor when you came over?

SHLINK: I was seven. I've worked ever since.

GARGA: You don't own anything else?

SHLINK: Not a thing.

GARGA *to the preacher:* I'll give you this man's property on
one condition. For the sake of the orphans and drunks
whose shelter this will be, you must let me spit in your
insufferable face.

PREACHER: I'm a man of God.

GARGA: Then take the consequences.

PREACHER: I have no right.

GARGA: Snow falls on the orphans, the drunks die like flies,
and you take care of your face.

PREACHER: I'm ready. I've kept my face clean; I'm twenty-
one. You must have your reasons I beg you to understand
me: please ask the lady to turn around.

MARY: I'll despise you if you accept.

PREACHER: I expect that. There are better faces than mine.
But none too good for this.

GARGA: Spit in his face, Shlink, if you please.

MARY: This isn't right, George. I don't like it.

GARGA: A tooth for a tooth, if you please.

*Shlink steps coolly up to the Preacher and spits in his face. Worm
bleats like a goat. The reformed sinner plays a drum roll.*

PREACHER *shaking his fists, in tears:* Excuse me.

GARGA *throws the papers at him:* Here is the deed of gift. For
the Salvation Army. And this is for you. *Gives him his gun.*
Now get out, you swine!

PREACHER: I thank you in the name of my mission. *He leaves,
bowing awkwardly. The hymn singing fades with striking speed.*

GARGA: You spoiled my fun. Your brutality has no equal.

I'll keep some of the money. But I'm not staying here, because this is the point of the whole thing, Mr Shlink from Yokohama: I'm going to Tahiti.

MARY: You're yellow, George. When the preacher left, you winced. I saw you. How desperate you are!

GARGA: I came here peeled to the bones. Trembling from the spiritual debauches of the last two weeks. I spat in his face many times. Each time he swallowed it. I despise him. It's all over.

MARY: Disgusting!

GARGA: You left me in the lurch. A tooth for a tooth.

MARY: And now you're going to carry on the fight with me? You never knew where to stop. God will punish you. I want nothing from you, only my peace.

GARGA: And to find bread for your parents in a whore's bed. And to offer your horse's smell for sale and say: It's not me! That you may prosper in bed and dwell long upon the earth. *He exits with the others.*

MARY: I don't really understand you, Mr Shlink. But you can go in all four directions, while others have only one. A man has many possibilities, hasn't he? I can see that a man has many possibilities. *Shlink shrugs his shoulders, turns around and leaves. Mary follows him.*

3

Living-room of the Garga Family

22 August, after 7 p.m.
A filthy attic. In the rear a curtain hangs in front of a small balcony. John Garga and his wife Mae. Manky is singing a song.

JOHN: Something has happened here that's hard to talk about.

MANKY: They say your son George is mixed up in the kind of

deal that never ends. They say he's mixed up with a yellow man. The yellow man has done something to him.

MAE: We can't interfere.

JOHN: If he's been fired, we can eat grass.

MAE: Ever since he was a little boy, he's had to have things his way.

MANKY: They say you shouldn't have hired out your daughter, Mary, to this yellow man.

MAE: Yes, Mary's been gone two weeks now too.

MANKY: People must be beginning to see that it all hangs together.

MAE: When our daughter left, she told us she'd been offered a job in a lumber business. Ten dollars a week and only linen to attend to.

MANKY: Linen for a yellow man!

JOHN: In cities like this nobody can see the next house. When people read a newspaper, they never know what it means.

MANKY: Or when they buy a ticket.

JOHN: When they ride in these electric trolleys, it probably gives them . . .

MANKY: Stomach cancer.

JOHN: Nobody knows. Here in the States wheat grows summer and winter.

MANKY: But suddenly, without any warning, there's no dinner for you. You walk in the street with your children, observing the fourth commandment to the letter, and suddenly you've only got your son's or daughter's hand in your hand, and your son and daughter themselves have sunk into a sudden gravel pit.

JOHN: Hello, who's there?

Garga stands in the doorway.

GARGA: Still chewing the fat?

JOHN: Have you finally got the money for the two weeks?

GARGA: Yes.

JOHN: Have you still got your job or not? A new jacket! Looks like you've been well paid for something? Huh?

There's your mother, George. *To Mae:* Why are you standing there like Lot's wife? Your son's here. Our son has come to take us out to dinner at the Metropolitan Bar. Your darling son looks pale, doesn't he? Slightly drunk maybe. Come on, Manky, let's go. We'll smoke our pipes on the stairs!

Both go out.

MAE: Tell me, George, are you mixed up with somebody?

GARGA: Has somebody been here?

MAE: No.

GARGA: I've got to go away.

MAE: Where?

GARGA: Any place. You always get scared at once.

MAE: Don't go away.

GARGA: I've got to. One man insults another. That's disagreeable for the man who gets insulted. But under certain circumstances the first man is willing to give up a whole lumber business for the pleasure of insulting the other. That's even more disagreeable for the second man. Maybe when he's been insulted like that, he'd better leave town. But since that might be too pleasant for him, even that may no longer be possible. In any case, he's got to be free.

MAE: Aren't you free?

GARGA: No. *Pause.* We're none of us free. It starts in the morning with our coffee, and we're beaten if we play the fool. A mother salts her children's food with her tears and washes their shirts with her sweat. And their future is secure until the Ice Age, and the root sits in their heart. And when you grow up and want to do something, body and soul, they pay you, brainwash you, label you, and sell you at a high price, and you're not even free to fail.

MAE: But tell me what's getting you down.

GARGA: You can't help me.

MAE: I can help you. Don't run away from your father. How are we going to live?

GARGA *giving her money:* I've been fired. But here's enough money for six months.

MAE: We're worried about not hearing from your sister. We hope she's still got her job.

GARGA: I don't know. I advised her to leave the yellow man.

MAE: I know you won't let me talk to you the way other mothers do.

GARGA: Oh, all those other people, the many good people, all the many other good people who stand at their lathes and earn their bread and make all the good tables for all the many good bread eaters; all the many good table makers and bread eaters with their many good families, so many, whole armies of them, and nobody spits in their soup, and nobody sends them into the next world with a good kick in the pants, and no flood comes over them to the tune of 'Stormy the night and the sea runs high'.[3]

MAE: Oh, George!

GARGA: No! Don't Oh, George me! I don't like it, and I don't want to hear it any more.

MAE: You don't want to hear it any more? But what about me? How am I to live? With these filthy walls and a stove that won't last through the winter.

GARGA: It's plain as day, Mother. Nothing can last long now, neither the stove nor the walls.

MAE: How can you say that? Are you blind?

GARGA: And neither will the bread in the cupboard or the dress on your back, and neither will your daughter for that matter.

MAE: Sure, go ahead and shout, so everybody can hear. How everything is useless and anything that takes an effort is too much and wears you down. But how am I to live? And I've still got so much time ahead of me.

GARGA: If it's as bad as all that, speak up. What makes it so bad?

MAE: You know.

GARGA: Yes, I know.

MAE: But the way you say that! What do you think I said? I won't have you looking at me like that. I gave you birth and fed you milk, I gave you bread and beat you, so don't look at me like that. A husband is what he wants to be, I won't say a word to him. He has worked for us.

GARGA: I want you to come with me.

MAE: What's that?

GARGA: Come south with me. I'll work, I can cut down trees. We'll build a log cabin and you'll cook for me. I need you terribly.

MAE: Who are you saying that to? The wind? When you come back, you can come by and see where we spent our last days. *Pause*. When are you leaving?

GARGA: Now.

MAE: Don't say anything to them. I'll get your things together and put your bundle under the stairs.

GARGA: Thank you.

MAE: Don't mention it.

Both go out.

Worm enters cautiously and sniffs around the room.

MANKY: Hey, who's there? *Comes in with John.*

WORM: Me, a gentleman. Mr Garga, I presume? Mr John Garga?

MANKY: What do you want?

WORM: Me? Nothing. Could I speak to your son – I mean, if he's had his bath?

JOHN: What's it all about?

WORM *sadly shaking his head:* What inhospitality! If it's not too much of an effort, could you tell me where your excellent son is taking his nap?

JOHN: He's gone away. Go to the devil. This isn't an information bureau.

Mae enters.

WORM: Too bad! Too bad! We miss your son terribly, sir. And it's about your daughter, too, in case you're interested.

MAE: Where is she?

WORM: In a Chinese hotel, milady, in a Chinese hotel.

JOHN: What?

MAE: Holy Mary!

MANKY: What's the meaning of this? What's she doing there?

WORM: Nothing, just eating. Mr Shlink wants me to tell you and your son that he should come and get her. She's too expensive, it's running into money, the lady's got a healthy appetite. She doesn't lift a finger. But she pursues us with immoral propositions. She's demoralizing the hotel. She'll have the police after us.

MAE: John!

WORM *shouting:* We're sick of her.

MAE: Christ!

MANKY: Where is she? I'll get her right away.

WORM: Sure, you'll get her. Are you a bird dog? How do you know where the hotel is? You young fool! It's not so simple. You should have kept an eye on the lady. It's all your son's fault. Tell him to call for the bitch and kindly look after her. Or tomorrow night we'll get the police on the move.

MAE: Good God. Just tell us where she is. I don't know where my son is. He's gone away. Don't be hard-hearted. Oh, Mary! John, plead with him. What's happened to Mary? What's happening to me? Oh, George! John, what a city this is! What people! *Goes out.*

Shlink appears in the doorway.

WORM *mutters in a fright:* Yes, I . . . this place has two entrances . . . *Sneaks out.*

SHLINK *simply:* My name is Shlink. I used to be a lumber dealer, now I catch flies. I'm all alone in the world. Can you rent me a place to sleep? I'll pay board. On the door plate downstairs I recognized the name of a man I know.

MANKY: Your name is Shlink? You're the man who's been holding these people's daughter.

SHLINK: Who's that?

JOHN: Mary Garga, sir. My daughter, Mary Garga.

SHLINK: Don't know her. I don't know your daughter.

JOHN: The gentleman who was just here . . .

MANKY: Sent by you, I presume.

JOHN: Who slipped away the moment you came in.

SHLINK: I don't know the gentleman.

JOHN: But you and my son . . .

SHLINK: You're making fun of a poor man. Of course there's no danger in insulting me. I've gambled away my fortune; often you don't know how these things happen.

MANKY: What I say is, when I steer my ship into port, I know my channel.

JOHN: You can't trust anybody.

SHLINK: Lonely through sheer bungling at an age when the ground must close if snow is not to fall into the crevices, I see you deserted by your breadwinner. I'm not without compassion; and if you'll keep me, my work will have a purpose.

JOHN: Reasons won't fill anybody's stomach. We're not beggars. We can't eat fish heads. But our hearts aren't made of stone, we feel for your loneliness. Your elbows want to rest on a family table. We're poor people.

SHLINK: I like everything, I can digest gravel.

JOHN: It's a small room. We're already packed in like sardines.

SHLINK: I can sleep on the floor, and a space half my length is good enough for me. I'm as happy as a child as long as my back's protected from the wind. I'll pay half the rent.

JOHN: All right, I understand. You don't want to wait out in the wind. You may share our roof.

MAE *comes in:* I've got to hurry downtown before dark.

JOHN: You're always gone when I need you. I'm taking this man in. He's lonely. There's room now that your son has run away. Shake hands with him.

MAE: Our home was on the prairies.

SHLINK: I know.

JOHN: What are you doing in the corner?

MAE: I'm making up my bed under the stairs.

JOHN: Where's your bundle?

SHLINK: I have nothing. I'll sleep on the stairs, ma'am. I won't intrude. My hand will never touch you. I know the skin on it is yellow.

MAE *coldly:* I'll give you mine.

SHLINK: I don't deserve it. I meant what I said. I know you didn't mean your skin. Forgive me.

MAE: I open the window over the stairs at night. *Goes out.*

JOHN: She's a good soul under that skin.

SHLINK: God bless her. I'm a simple man, don't expect words from my mouth. I've only teeth in it.

4

Chinese Hotel

The Morning of 24 August
Skinny, Baboon and Jane.

SKINNY *in the doorway:* Aren't you even thinking of starting a new business?

BABOON *lying in a hammock, shakes his head:* All the boss does is walk along the waterfront, checking the passengers on the ships bound for Tahiti. Some fellow has run off with his soul and his entire fortune, maybe to Tahiti. It's him he's looking for. He's brought what was left of his belongings for safekeeping, down to the last cigar butt. *Referring to Jane:* And he's been feeding this here free of charge for the last three weeks. He's even taken the fellow's sister in. What he means to do with her is a mystery to me. He often sits up all night, talking to her.

SKINNY: You've let him put you out in the street, and now you feed him and his hangers-on too?

BABOON: He makes a few dollars hauling coal, but he gives them to the fellow's family; he's taken up lodging with them, but he can't live there, they don't like having him around. That fellow really took him for a ride. He got himself a cheap trip to Tahiti and hung a tree trunk over the boss's head that's likely to come crashing down any minute;

because in five months at the most they're going to drag him into court for selling the same lumber twice.

SKINNY: And you bother to feed a wreck like that?

BABOON: He had to have his little joke. A man like him can always get credit. If that fellow stays lost, the boss will be back at the top of the lumber business in three months.

JANE *half dressed, making up:* I've always thought I'd end up like this: in a Chinese flophouse.

BABOON: You've no idea what's in store for you.

Two voices are heard from behind a screen.

MARY: Why don't you ever touch me? Why are you always wearing that smoky sack? I've got a suit for you, like other men wear. I can't sleep; I love you.

JANE: Pst! Listen! You can hear them again.

SHLINK: I am unworthy. I don't know anything about virgins. And I've been conscious of the smell of my race for years.

MARY: Yes, it's a bad smell. Yes, it's bad.

SHLINK: Why cut yourself in pieces like that? Look: My body is numb, it even affects my skin. Man's skin in its natural state is too thin for this world, that's why people do their best to make it thicker.[4] The method would be satisfactory if the growth could be stopped. A piece of leather, for instance, stays the way it is, but a man's skin grows, it gets thicker and thicker.

MARY: Is it because you can't find an opponent?

SHLINK: In the first stage a table has edges; later on, and that's the nasty part of it, the same table is like rubber, but in the thick-skinned stage there's neither table nor rubber.

MARY: How long have you had this disease?

SHLINK: Since I was a boy on the rowboats on the Yangtze Kiang. The Yangtze tortured the junks and the junks tortured us. There was a man who trampled our faces every time he stepped into the boat. At night we were too lazy to move our faces away. Somehow the man was never too lazy. We in turn had a cat to torture. She was drowned while learning to swim, though she'd eaten the rats that were all over us. All those people had the disease.

MARY: When were you on the Yangtze Kiang?

SHLINK: We lay in the reeds in the early morning and felt the disease growing.

WORM *enters:* The wind has swallowed the fellow. There's neither hide nor hair of him in all Chicago.

SHLINK: You'd better get some sleep. *Steps out.* Still no news?

Shlink goes out; through the open door the sound of Chicago waking is heard, the shouts of the milkmen, the rumbling of meat waggons.

MARY: Chicago is waking up. The shouting of milkmen, the rumbling of meat waggons, the newspapers and the fresh morning air. It would be good to go away, it's good to wash in water, there's something good about the prairie and the asphalt.[5] Right now, for instance, there's surely a cool wind in the prairies where we used to live.

BABOON: Do you still know your shorter catechism, Jane?

JANE *droning:* Things are getting worse, things are getting worse, things are getting worse.

They begin to straighten the room, pull up the blinds, and stand the sleeping mats up.

MARY: For my part, I'm a little out of breath. I want to sleep with a man and I don't know how. Some women are like dogs, yellow and black ones. But I can't do it. I'm all torn apart. These walls are like paper. You can't breathe. You've got to set it all on fire. Where are the matches, a black box, to make the water come in. Oh, if I swim away, I'll be in two parts, swimming in two different directions.

JANE: Where has he gone?

BABOON: He's looking into the faces of all the people who are leaving town because Chicago's too cruel.

JANE: There's an east wind. The Tahiti-bound ships are weighing anchor.

5

Same Hotel

A month later, 19 or 20 September
A filthy bedroom. A hall. A glass-enclosed bar. Worm, George Garga, Manky and Baboon.

WORM *from the hall towards the bar:* He never sailed after all. The harpoon is in deeper than we thought. We thought the earth had swallowed him up. But now he's in Shlink's room, licking his wounds.

GARGA *in the bedroom:* That dog Shlink. 'In my dreams I call him my infernal bridegroom.[6] We are parted from bed and board, he has no room any more. His little bride smokes stogies, and tucks money away in her stocking.' That's me! *Laughs.*

MANKY *in the bar behind the glass partition:* Life is strange. I knew a man who was really tops, but he loved a woman. Her family was starving. He had two thousand dollars, but he let them starve before his eyes. Because with those two thousand dollars he loved the woman, without them he couldn't get her. That was infamous, but he can't be held responsible.

GARGA: 'Behold, I am a sinner. I loved deserts, burnt orchards, run-down shops, and hot drinks.[7] You are mistaken. I am a little man.' I'm through with Mr Shlink from Yokohama.

BABOON: Take that lumber dealer. He never had any heart. But one day a passion made him wreck his whole lumber business. And now he's hauling coal down there. He had the whole neighbourhood by the throat.

WORM: We took him in the way you might take in an exhausted pedigree dog. But now by some stroke of luck his lost bone has turned up again, and if he won't let it go our patience will be at an end.

GARGA: 'One day I'll be his widow. That day, I know, has already been marked on the calendar. And I in clean under-wear shall walk behind his corpse, swinging my legs lustily in the warm sun.'[8]

MARY *enters with a lunch basket:* George.

GARGA: Who's that? *Recognizing her.* Good God! You look like a soiled rag!

MARY: I know.

WORM *in the direction of the bar:* He's dead drunk. And now his sister has come to see him. He's told her that she's soiled. Where's the old man?

BABOON: He's coming today. I've brought Jane. For bait, I suppose. There won't be any punches pulled in this fight.

JANE *shakes her head:* I don't understand you. Give me a drink. Gin.

MARY: I'm glad to see you had a better opinion of me. Or you wouldn't be surprised to see me here now. Besides, I remind you of the days when you were the pride of women, dancing the shimmy and ragtime with a crease in your pants on Saturday night, when your only vices were tobacco, whisky and the love of women, the legitimate vices of men. I wish you'd think of that, George. *Pause.* How do you live?

GARGA *lightly:* It gets cold here at night. Do you need any-thing? Are you hungry?

MARY *lightly, shaking her head and looking at him:* Oh, George, we've had vultures over our heads for some time now.

GARGA *lightly:* When were you home last? *Mary is silent.* I heard you were spending your time around here.

MARY: Is that so? I wonder who's looking after them at home.

GARGA *coldly:* You needn't worry. I've heard that some-body's taking care of them. And I know what you've been doing. And I know something about a certain Chinese hotel too.

MARY: Does it make you feel good to be so cold-hearted, George?

Garga looks at her.

MARY: Don't look at me like that. I know you expect a confession.

GARGA: Go ahead!

MARY: I love him. Why don't you say something?

GARGA: Go ahead and love him. That will weaken him.

MARY: For God's sake, stop looking at the ceiling. I can't win him.

GARGA: That's disgraceful.

MARY: I know. – Oh, George, I'm torn in two. Because I can't win him. I tremble under my dress when I see him and I say the wrong thing.

GARGA: I can't tell you the right thing. A rejected woman! I had one once who wasn't worth a bottle of rum, but she knew how to attract men. She got paid for it too. And she knew her power.

MARY: You say such biting things. They swim in my head like gin. But are they good? You ought to know if they're good. But I understand you now.

Shlink enters the hall.

WORM: I can tell you from experience: humanity has fallen fists over calluses for a lot of paper dreams. And nothing is so much like paper as real life. *Mary Garga turns round and bumps into Shlink.*

SHLINK: You here, Miss Garga?

MARY: It's considered wrong for a woman to tell a man she loves him. But I'd like to tell you that my love for you doesn't prove a thing. I don't want anything from you. It's not easy for me to tell you that. Maybe you knew it all along.

GARGA *comes out of the bedroom:* Stay here, Mary. We've got the prairies written on our faces, and here we've been tossed into the city. Don't hold back. Do what you want to do.

MARY: Yes, George.

GARGA: He works like a horse, and I lie lazily in a pool of absinthe.

SHLINK: The men who conquer the world like to lie on their backs.

GARGA: And those who own it work.

SHLINK: Are you worried?

GARGA *to Shlink:* Every time I look at you, you're sizing me up. Have you backed the wrong horse? Your face has grown old.

SHLINK: Thank you for not forgetting me. I was beginning to think you had gone south. Forgive me. I have taken the liberty of supporting your unfortunate family with the work of my hands.

GARGA: Is that true, Mary? I didn't know that. You've wormed your way in? You're vile enough to support my family, and you enjoy it? You hand me a laugh. *Goes left into the bedroom, lies down, and laughs.*

SHLINK *follows him:* Go ahead and laugh, I like to hear you laugh. Your laughter is my sunshine, it was misery here. It's been dismal without you. It's been three weeks, Garga.

GARGA: I've been satisfied, all in all.

SHLINK: Of course. You've been rolling in clover.

GARGA: Only my back is getting thin as a rail from lying on it.

SHLINK: How pitiful life is! You're rolling in clover and the clover's not sweet enough.

GARGA: I expect more out of life than to wear my shoes out kicking you.

SHLINK: Kindly take no notice of my insignificant person or my intentions. But I'm still here. If you have to quit, you won't leave the ring in innocence.

GARGA: I'm quitting, though. I'm going on strike. I throw in the towel. Have I sunk my teeth so deep into you? You're a small hard betel nut, I ought to spit it out, I know it's harder than my teeth and that it's only a shell.

SHLINK *pleased:* I'm doing my best to give you all the light you need. I show myself in every possible light, Mr Garga. *Goes under the lamp.*

GARGA: You want to auction off your pock-marked soul? Are you hardened to all suffering? Utterly callous?

SHLINK: Crack the nut.

GARGA: You're withdrawing into my corner. You're staging a metaphysical fight, but leaving a slaughterhouse behind you.

SHLINK: You mean this business with your sister? I haven't butchered anything your hands protected.

GARGA: I have only two hands. Whatever is human to me you devour like a chunk of meat. You open my eyes to possible sources of help by choking them off. You use my family to help yourself. You live on my reserves. I'm getting thinner and thinner. I'm getting metaphysical. And on top of everything, you vomit all this in my face.

MARY: Please, George, can't I go now? *She retreats towards the rear.*

GARGA *pulling her forward:* No, certainly not! We've just started talking about you. I've just noticed you.

SHLINK: It's my misfortune to tread on delicate ground. I'll retreat. You're never aware of your affections until their objects are in the morgue, and I feel the need of acquainting you with your affections. But please proceed, I understand you perfectly.

GARGA: But I am making sacrifices. Have I refused?

MARY: Let me go. I'm afraid.

GARGA: This way, sir. *Runs into the hall.* Let's start a family!

MARY: George!

GARGA: Stay here! *In the direction of the bedroom.* I demand a little human involvement on your part, sir.

SHLINK: I wouldn't say no for a minute.

GARGA: You love this man? And he's indifferent? *Mary weeps.*

SHLINK: I hope you're not overestimating your power. *Runs back to the bedroom.*

GARGA: Don't worry. This will be a step forward. Let's see

now, this is Thursday night. This is the Chinese hotel and this is my sister, Mary Garga. *Runs out.* Come here, Mary. My sister. This is Mr Shlink from Yokohama. He has something to tell you.

MARY: George!

GARGA *goes out to get drinks:* 'I fled into the outskirts of the city, where women with crooked orange mouths cower white in glowing thorn bushes.'

MARY: It's dark in the window and I want to go home now.

SHLINK: I'll go with you if you like.

GARGA: 'Their hair was black-lacquered shells, ever so thin, their eyes were dulled by the winds of debauch in the drunken night and by sacrifices in the open fields.'

MARY *softly:* Please don't ask me that.

GARGA: 'Their thin dresses, like iridescent snake skins drenched with never-ending rain slapped against their for ever excited limbs.'

SHLINK: I meant it when I asked you. I have no secrets from anyone.

GARGA: 'They cover their legs to the very toenails, which are incrusted with molten copper; the madonna in the clouds turns pale at the sight of her sisters.' *Comes back, hands Shlink a glass.* Won't you drink? I find it necessary.

SHLINK: Why do you drink? Drinkers lie.[9]

GARGA: It's fun talking with you. When I drink, half my thoughts float downward. I guide them to the ground and then they seem lighter. Drink!

SHLINK: I'd rather not. But if you insist.

GARGA: I'm inviting you to drink with me and you refuse.

SHLINK: I don't refuse, but my brain is all I've got.

GARGA *after a moment:* Forgive me, let's go halves: You'll turn off your brain. When you've drunk, you'll make love.

SHLINK *drinks as in a ritual:* When I have drunk, I'll make love.

GARGA *calls from the bedroom:* Won't you have a drink, Mary? No? Why don't you sit down?

BABOON: Shut up. I could hear them talking before. Now they're not saying anything.

GARGA *to Mary:* This is the Black Pit. Forty years are passing. I don't say no. The ground is giving way, the water of the sewers rises to the surface, but the tide of their lusts is too weak. For four hundred years I have dreamed of mornings on the ocean, I had the salt wind in my eyes. How smooth it was! *He drinks.*

SHLINK *submissively:* I ask you for your hand, Miss Garga. Shall I throw myself humbly at your feet? Please come with me. I love you.

MARY *runs into the bar:* Help! They're selling me!

MANKY: Here I am, beautiful!

MARY: I knew you'd be wherever I am.

GARGA: 'Like at the opera, a breeze opens gaps in the partitions.'[10]

SHLINK *bellowing:* Will you kindly come out of the bar, Mary Garga! *Mary comes out of the bar.* I beg you, don't throw yourself away, Miss Garga.

MARY: All I want is a little room with nothing in it. I've stopped wanting very much, Pat, I promise you that I never will again.

GARGA: Fight for your chance, Shlink.

SHLINK: Think of the years that won't pass, Mary Garga, and think how sleepy you are.

MANKY: Come with me, I've got four hundred pounds, that means a roof in the winter and no more ghosts except in the morgues.

SHLINK: I implore you, Mary Garga, come with me. I shall treat you like my wife and wait on you and hang myself without any fuss if ever I hurt you.

GARGA: He's not lying. I promise you that. That's what you'll get if you go with him. Down to the last cent. *Goes into the bar.*

MARY: Tell me, Pat, even if I don't love you, do you love me?

MANKY: I think so, beautiful. And it's not written anywhere between heaven and earth that you don't love me.

GARGA: Is that you, Jane? Polishing off the cocktails? You don't look exactly yourself. Have you sold everything?

JANE: Get rid of him, Baboon. I can't stand his face. He's molesting me. Even if I'm not living in milk and honey these days, I don't have to put up with ridicule.

BABOON: I'll crack the nose of any man who says you're an old shoe.

GARGA: Did they feed you too? Your face looks like a lemon ice that's been left standing. Damn it all, you used to wear glad rags like an opera singer, and now you look as if they'd sprinkled you with black powder. But I'll say this much: you didn't come of your own accord when only the flies made spots on you, my drunken chick.

MARY: Let's go, then. I'd have gladly obliged you, Shlink, but I can't. It's not pride.

SHLINK: Stay if you like. I won't repeat my offer if it displeases you. But don't let the pit swallow you up. There are many places to get away from a man.

GARGA: Not for a woman. Forget it, Shlink. Don't you see what she's driving at? If you'd preferred a roof in the winter, Jane, you'd still be sewing shirts.

SHLINK: Drink before you make love, Mary Garga.

MARY: Come, Pat. This isn't a good place. Is this your woman, George? Is she? I'm glad I had a chance to see her. *Out with Manky.*

SHLINK *calls after her:* I won't forsake you. Come back when you've found out.

BABOON: An old shoe, gentlemen, well worn. *He laughs.*

GARGA *shining a candle in Shlink's face:* Your face is in good shape. But where does your good will get me?

SHLINK: The sacrifices on both sides have been considerable. How many ships do you need to get to Tahiti? Do you want me to hoist my shirt for a sail, or your sister's? I hold you responsible for your sister's fate. You showed her that men would always treat her as an object. I haven't spoiled anything for you, I hope. I almost got her as a virgin, but you wanted me to have left-overs. And don't forget your family

that you're abandoning. Now you've seen what you are
sacrificing.

GARGA: I want to slaughter them all now. I know that. I
think I'll get the jump on you. And now I understand why
you've fattened them on what you earn hauling coal. I
won't let you do me out of my fun. And now I'm taking
delivery of this little animal that you've been keeping for
me.

JANE: I refuse to be insulted. I stand on my own feet, I
support myself.

GARGA: And now I request you to hand over the money you
made selling that lumber twice. I hope you've been keeping
it for me. The time has come.

Shlink takes out the money and gives it to Garga.

GARGA: I'm dead drunk. But drunk or sober, I've got a good
idea, Shlink, a very good idea. *Goes out with Jane.*

BABOON: That was your last money, sir. And where did it
come from? They'll be asking you about it. Broost & Co.
have demanded delivery of the lumber they paid for.

SHLINK *not listening to him:* A chair. *They have occupied the
chairs and do not stand up.* My rice and water.

WORM: There's no more rice for you, sir. Your account is
overdrawn.

6

Lake Michigan

The end of September
Woods: Shlink and Mary.

MARY: The trees look draped in human dung, the sky is
close enough to touch, but what is it to me? I'm cold. I'm
like a half-frozen quail. I can't help myself.

SHLINK: If it will do you any good, I love you.

MARY: I've thrown myself away. Why has my love turned to bitter fruit? Others have their summer when they love, but I'm withering away and tormenting myself. My body is soiled.

SHLINK: Tell me how low you feel. It will relieve you.

MARY: I lay in bed with a man who was like an animal. My whole body was numb, but I gave myself to him, many times, and I couldn't get warm. He smoked stogies in between, a seaman. I loved you every hour I spent between those papered walls, I was so obsessed that he thought it was love and wanted to stop me. I slept into the black darkness. I don't owe you anything, but my conscience cries out to me that I've soiled my body, which is yours even if you scorned it.

SHLINK: I'm sorry you're cold. I thought the air was warm and dark. I don't know what the men of this country say to the women they love. If it will do you any good: I love you.

MARY: I'm such a coward, my courage has gone with my innocence.

SHLINK: You'll wash yourself clean.

MARY: Maybe I ought to go down to the water, but I can't. I'm not ready yet. Oh, this despair! This heart that won't be appeased! I'm never anything more than half, I can't even love, it's only vanity. I hear what you say, I have ears and I'm not deaf, but what does it mean? Maybe I'm asleep, they'll come and wake me, and maybe it's just that I'd do the most shameful things to get a roof over my head, that I lie to myself and close my eyes.

SHLINK: Come, it's getting cold.

MARY: But the leaves are warm and shelter us from the sky that's too close. *They go out.*

MANKY *enters:* Her tracks point this way. You need a good sense of humour in a September like this. The crayfish are mating, the rutting cry of the deer is heard in the thicket, and the badger season is open. But my flippers are cold and

I've wrapped my black stumps in newspaper. Where can she be living? That's the worst of it. If she's lying around like a fishbone in that greasy saloon, she'll never have a clean petticoat again. Only stains. Oh, Pat Mankyboddle, I'm going to court-martial you. Too weak to defend myself, I'd better attack. I'll devour the no-good with skin and bones, I'll speed up my digestion with prayers, the vultures will be shot at sunrise and hung up in the Mankyboddle Museum. Brrr! Words! Toothless phrases! *He takes a revolver from his pocket.* This is the coldest answer! Stalk through the jungle looking for a woman, will you, you old swine! Down on all fours! Damn, this underbrush is suicide. Watch yourself, Paddy. Where can a woman go when it's all up with her? Let her go, Paddy boy, have a smoke, take a bite to eat, put that thing away. Forward, march! *Goes out.*

MARY *coming back with Shlink:* It's loathsome before God and man. I won't go with you.

SHLINK: Mouldy sentiments. Air out your soul.

MARY: I can't. You're making a sacrifice of me.

SHLINK: You've always got to have your head in some man's armpits, no matter whose.

MARY: I'm nothing to you.

SHLINK: You can't live alone.

MARY: You took me so quickly, as if you were afraid I'd get away. Like a sacrifice.

SHLINK: You ran into the bushes like a rabid bitch and now you're running out again like a rabid bitch.

MARY: Am I what you say? I'm always what you say. I love you. Never forget that, I love you. I love you like a bitch in heat. That's what you said. But now pay me. Yes, I'm in the mood to get paid. Give me your money, I'll live on it. I'm a whore.

SHLINK: Something wet is running down your face. What kind of a whore is that?

MARY: Don't make fun of me, just give me the money. Don't look at me. It's not tears that make my face wet, it's the fog.

Shlink gives her paper money. I won't thank you, Mr Shlink
from Yokohama. It's a straight business deal, no need for
thanks.

SHLINK: You'd better be going. You won't make money
here. *Goes out.*

7

The Garga Family's Living-room

29 September 1912
*The room is full of new furniture. John Garga, Mae, George, Jane,
Manky, all dressed in new clothes for the wedding dinner.*

JOHN: Ever since that man we don't like to speak of, who has
a different skin but who goes down to the coal yards to
work night and day for a family he knows; ever since the
man in the coal yards with the different skin has been watching over us, things have been getting better for us every day,
in every way. Today, without knowing of the wedding,
he's made it possible for our son George to have a wedding
worthy of the director of a big business. New ties, black
suits, the breath of whisky on our lips – amid new furniture.

MAE: Isn't it strange that the man in the coal yards should
make so much hauling coal?

GARGA: I make the money.

MAE: From one day to the next you decided to get married.
Wasn't it a little sudden, Jane?

JANE: The snow melts, and where is it then? And you can
pick the wrong man, it often happens.

MAE: Right man, wrong man, that's not the question. The
question is whether you stick to him.

JOHN: Nonsense! Eat your steak and give the bride your
hand.

GARGA *takes Jane by the wrist:* It's a good hand. I'm all right here. Let the wallpaper peel, I've got new clothes, I eat steak, I can taste the plaster, I've got half an inch of mortar all over me, I see a piano. Hang a wreath on the picture of our dear sister, Mary Garga, born twenty years ago on the prairies. Put everlastings under glass. It's good to sit here, good to lie here, the black wind doesn't come in here.

JANE *stands up:* What's the matter, George? Have you a fever?

GARGA: I feel fine in my fever, Jane.

JANE: I keep wondering what your plans are for me, George.

GARGA: Why are you so pale, mother? Isn't your prodigal son back again under your roof? Why are you all standing against the wall like plaster statues?

MAE: Perhaps because of the fight you keep talking about.

GARGA: It's only flies in my brain. I can shoo them away. *Shlink enters.* Mother, get a steak and a glass of whisky for our welcome guest. I was married this morning. My dear wife, tell him!

JANE: Fresh out of bed this morning, my husband and I went to the sheriff and said: Can we be married here? He said: I know you, Jane – will you always stay with your husband? But I saw that he was a good man with a beard, he had nothing against me, so I said: Life isn't exactly the way you think.

SHLINK: Congratulations, Garga. You're a vindictive man.

GARGA: There's a hideous fear in your smile! For good reason. Don't eat too fast. You have plenty of time. Where's Mary? I hope she's being taken care of. Your satisfaction must be complete. Unfortunately there's no chair for you at the moment, Shlink. We're one chair short. Otherwise our furnishings are new and complete. Look at the piano. A delightful place. I mean to spend my evenings here with my family. I've started a new life. Tomorrow I'm going back to C. Maynes's lending library.

MAE: Oh, George, aren't you talking too much?

GARGA: Do you hear that? My family doesn't want me to

have anything more to do with you. Our acquaintance is at an end, Mr Shlink. It has been most profitable. The furniture speaks for itself. My family's wardrobe speaks loud and clear. There's plenty of cash. I thank you.

Silence.

SHLINK: May I ask just one favour of you? A personal matter. I have a letter here from the firm of Broost & Co. It bears the seal of the Attorney-General of the State of Virginia. I haven't opened it yet. You would oblige me by doing so. Any news, even the worst, would be more acceptable to me from your lips. *Garga reads the letter.* Of course this is my own private affair, but a hint from you would make things much easier for me.

MAE: Why don't you say something, George? What are you planning to do, George? You look as if you were planning something. There's nothing that frightens me more. You men hide behind your unknown thoughts as if they were smoke. And we wait like cattle before slaughter. You say: wait a while, you go away, you come back, and you're unrecognizable. And we don't know what you've done to yourselves. Tell me your plan, and if you don't know what it is, admit it, so I'll know what to do. I've got to plan my life too. Four years in this city of steel and dirt! Oh, George!

GARGA: You see, the bad years were the best, and now they're over. Don't say anything to me. You, my parents, and you, Jane, my wife, I've decided to go to jail.

JOHN: What are you saying? Is that where your money comes from? It was written on your face when you were five years old that you'd end up in jail. I never asked what went on between the two of you, I knew it was rotten. You've both lost the ground from under your feet. Buying pianos and going to jail, dragging in whole armloads of steak and robbing a family of its livelihood is all the same to you. Where's Mary, your sister? *He tears off his jacket and throws it on the floor.* There's my jacket, I never wanted to put it on. But I'm used to the kind of humiliations this city still has in store for me.

JANE: How long will it be, George?

SHLINK *to John:* Some lumber was sold twice. Naturally that means jail, because the sheriff isn't interested in the circumstances. I, your friend, could explain certain things to the sheriff as neatly and simply as Standard Oil explains its tax returns. I am prepared to listen to your son, Mrs Garga.

JANE: Don't let them talk you into anything, George, do what you see fit, regardless. I, your wife, will keep the house running while you're gone.

JOHN *laughing loudly:* She's going to keep the house running! A girl who was picked off the streets only yesterday. We're to be fed by the wages of sin!

SHLINK *to George:* You've given me to understand that your family means a great deal to you. You'd like to spend your evenings among this furniture. You'll have a thought or two for me, your friend, who is busy making things easier for you all. I am prepared to save you for your family's sake.

MAE: You can't go to jail, George.

GARGA: I know you don't understand, Mother. It's so hard to harm a man, to destroy him is utterly impossible. The world is too poor. We wear ourselves out cluttering it with things to fight about.

JANE *to Garga:* There you go philosophizing with the roof rotting over our heads.

GARGA *to Shlink:* Search the whole world, you'll find ten evil men and not one evil action. Only trifles can destroy a man. No, I'm through. I'll draw a line under the account, and then I'll go.

SHLINK: Your family would like to know if they mean anything to you. If you won't hold them up, they'll fall. One little word, Garga!

GARGA: I give you all your freedom.

SHLINK: They'll rot, and you'll be to blame. There aren't many of them left. They might take a notion, just like you, to make a clean sweep, to cut up the dirty tablecloth and shake the cigar butts out of their clothes. The whole lot of

them might decide to imitate you, to be free and indecent,
with slobber on their shirts.

MAE: Be still, George, everything he says is true.

GARGA: Now at last, if I half close my eyes, I see certain
things in a cold light. Not your face, Mr Shlink, maybe you
haven't got one.

SHLINK: Forty years have been written off as so much dirt,
and now there will be a great freedom.

GARGA: That's how it is. The snow tried to fall, but it was
too cold. My family will eat left-overs again, and again
they'll be hungry. But I, I will strike down my enemy.

JOHN: All I see is weakness, nothing else. Since the day I first
laid eyes on you. Go ahead and leave us. Why shouldn't
they take the furniture away?

GARGA: I've read that feeble waters erode whole mountains.
And I still want to see your face, Shlink, your damned
invisible, frosted-glass face.

SHLINK: I have no desire to talk with you any further. Three
years. For a young man that's no more than a swing of the
door. But for me! I've drawn no profit from you if that's
any comfort to you. But you're not leaving a trace of sad-
ness in me, now that I'm going back into the noisy city to
carry on my business as I did before we met. *Exit.*

GARGA: All that remains for me to do now is phone the
police. *Exit.*

JANE: I'm going to the Chinese bar. I can do without the
police. *Exit.*

MAE: Sometimes I think Mary will never come back either.

JOHN: She has only herself to blame. Can we be expected to
help them when they live in vice?

MAE: Is there any better time to help them?

JOHN: Don't talk so much.

MAE *sits down next to him:* I wanted to ask you: what are you
going to do now?

JOHN: Me? Nothing. This part of our life is over.

MAE: You understand, don't you, what George is going to do
to himself?

JOHN: Yes. More or less. It won't help us any.

MAE: And what are you going to live on?

JOHN: On the money that's still left. And we'll sell the piano.

MAE: They'll take it away, it was come by dishonestly.

JOHN: Maybe we'll go back to Ohio. We'll do something.

MAE *stands up:* There's something else I wanted to tell you,
John, but I can't. I've never believed that a man could
suddenly be damned. It's decided in heaven. This is a day
like any other, and nothing has changed, but from this day
on you're damned.

JOHN: What are you going to do?

MAE: I'm going to do a certain thing, John, something I
want very much to do. Don't imagine I have any special
reason. But first I'll put some coal on the fire, you'll find
your supper in the kitchen. *Goes out.*

JOHN: Take care that the ghost of a shark doesn't eat you on
the stairs.

WAITER *enters:* Mrs Garga has ordered you a grog. Do you
wish to drink it in the dark, or should I put the light on?

JOHN: What do you think? Give us some light. *The waiter goes
out.*

MARY *enters:* Don't make any speeches. I've brought money.

JOHN: You dare to set foot here? A fine family. And look at
you!

MARY: I look fine. But where did you get all this new furniture? Have you taken in some money? I've taken in some
money too.

JOHN: Where did you get the money?

MARY: Do you really want to know?

JOHN: Give it here. You people have brought me to this
with hunger.

MARY: So you're taking my money? In spite of your new
furniture? Where's Mother?

JOHN: Deserters are stood up against the wall.

MARY: Did you send her out on the streets?

JOHN: Be cynical, wallow in the gutter, drink grog. But I'm
your father, you can't let me starve.

MARY: Where has she gone?

JOHN: You can go, too. I'm used to being left.

MARY: When did she leave here?

JOHN: At the end of my life I'm condemned to being poor and licking my children's spittle, but I won't have any truck with vice. I have no hesitation about throwing you out.

MARY: Give me back my money. It wasn't meant for you.

JOHN: Not a chance. You can sew me up in a shroud, I'll still beg for a pound of tobacco.

MARY: So long. *Goes out.*

JOHN: They've no more to say to a man than can be said in five minutes. Then they run out of lies. *Pause.* Actually everything there is to say could be covered in two minutes of silence.

GARGA *comes back:* Where's mother? Gone? Did she think I wasn't coming back up again? *He runs out and comes back.* She won't be back, she's taken her other dress. *He sits down at the table and writes a letter:* 'To *The Examiner.* I wish to call your attention to C. Shlink, the Malay lumber dealer. This man molested my wife, Jane Garga, and raped my sister, Mary Garga, who was in his employ. George Garga.' I won't say anything about my mother.

JOHN: That wipes out our family.

GARGA: I've written this letter. I'll put it in my pocket and forget the whole business. And in three years – that's how long they'll hold me – a week before I'm discharged, I'll send my letter to the newspaper. This man will be exterminated from this city, and when I come back he'll have vanished from my sight. But for him the day of my release will be marked by the howling of the lynch mobs.

8

C. Shlink's Private Office

20 October 1915, 1 p.m.
Shlink and a young clerk.

SHLINK *dictating:* Write to Miss Mary Garga, who has applied for a position as secretary, that I will never again have anything to do with either her or her family. To Standard Real Estate. Dear Sirs: As of today not a single share of our stock is in the hands of any outside firm and our business situation is secure. Consequently, there is nothing to prevent us from accepting your offer of a five-year contract.

AN EMPLOYEE *brings a man in:* This is Mr Shlink.

THE MAN: I've got three minutes to give you some information. You've got two minutes to understand your situation. Half an hour ago *The Examiner* received a letter from one of the state penitentiaries, signed by one Garga, showing you've committed a number of crimes. In five minutes the reporters will be here. You owe me a thousand dollars. *Shlink gives him the money. The man goes out.*

SHLINK *carefully packing his suitcase:* Carry on the business as long as you can. Mail these letters. I'll be back. *Goes out quickly.*

9

Bar Across the Street from the Prison

28 October 1915
Worm, Baboon, the Pugnosed Man, the Salvation Army Preacher,
Jane, Mary Garga. Noise from outside.

BABOON: Do you hear the howling of the lynch mob? These
are dangerous days for Chinatown. A week ago the crimes
of a Malayan lumber dealer came to light. Three years ago
he sent a man to prison, for three years the man kept quiet,
but a week before his release he wrote a letter to *The
Examiner*, telling the whole story.

THE PUGNOSED MAN: The human heart!

BABOON: The Malay himself, naturally, has skipped town.
But he's done for.

WORM: You can't say that about anybody. Consider the con-
ditions on this planet. A man never gets finished off all at
once, but at least a hundred times. A man has too many
possibilities. For instance, let me tell you the story of
G. Wishu, the bulldog man. But I'll need the nickelodeon.
The nickelodeon is played. This is the story of the dog, George
Wishu. George Wishu was born on the Emerald Isle. When
he was eighteen months old a fat man took him to the great
city of London. His own country let him go like a stranger.
In London he soon fell into the hands of a cruel woman,
who subjected him to gruesome tortures. After much
suffering he ran away to the country, where he was hunted
down between green hedges. Men shot at him with big
dangerous guns, and strange dogs chased him. He lost a leg
and from then on he limped. After several of his under-
takings had failed, weary of life and half starved, he found
refuge with an old man who shared his bread with him.
Here, after a life full of disappointments and adventures, he

died at the age of seven and a half with great serenity and composure. He lies buried in Wales. – Now tell me, sir, how are you going to fit all that under one roof?

THE PUGNOSED MAN: Who is this man that's wanted?

WORM: It's the Malay they're looking for. He went bankrupt once before, but in three years he managed by all sorts of dodges to recover his lumber business, and that made him a lot of enemies in his neighbourhood. But no court could have touched him if a man in jail hadn't brought his sex crimes to light. *To Jane:* Exactly when is your husband getting out?

JANE: Yes, that's it: I knew it a while ago. Gentlemen, don't go thinking that I don't know. It's on the twenty-eighth, yesterday or today.

BABOON: Cut the comedy, Jane.

THE PUGNOSED MAN: And who's that woman in the indecent dress?

BABOON: That's the victim, the sister of the man in jail.

JANE: Yes, that's my sister-in-law. She pretends not to know me, but when I was married she never came home a single night.

BABOON: The Malay ruined her.

THE PUGNOSED MAN: What's she dropping into the sink behind the bar?

WORM: I can't see. She's saying something, too. Keep still, Jane.

MARY *lets a banknote flutter into the sink:* When I held the bills in my hand that day, I saw God's eye watching me. I said: I've done everything for him. God turned away, there was a sound like tobacco fields rustling in the wind. I kept them, though. One bill! Another! Pieces of myself! I'm giving my purity away. Now the money's gone! I don't feel any better . . .

GARGA *enters with C. Maynes and three other men:* I've asked you to come with me so you could see with your own eyes that I've been done an injustice. I've brought you with me, Mr Maynes, to witness the kind of place I find my wife in after three years of absence. *He leads the men to the table where Jane is sitting.* Hello, Jane. How are you?

JANE: George! Is this the twenty-eighth? I didn't know. I'd have been home. Did you notice how cold it is there? Did you guess I'd be sitting here just to get warm?

GARGA: This is Mr Maynes. You know him. I'm going back to work in his store. And these are neighbours who take an interest in my situation.

JANE: How do you do, gentlemen. Oh, George, it's awful for me that I missed your day. What will you gentlemen think of me? Ken Si, wait on the gentlemen.

BARMAN *to the Pugnosed Man:* That's the fellow from the pen who informed on him.

GARGA: Hello, Mary. Have you been waiting for me? My sister's here too, as you can see.

MARY: Hello, George. Are you all right?

GARGA: Let's go home, Jane.

JANE: Oh, George, you're just saying that. But if I go with you, you'll scold me when we get home. I'd better tell you right away that the housework hasn't been done.

GARGA: I know that.

JANE: That's mean of you.

GARGA: I'm not chiding you, Jane. We're going to make a fresh start. My fight is finished. I've driven my opponent from the city, and that's the end of it.

JANE: No, George. Things will keep getting worse and worse. People say things are going to get better, but they keep getting worse, they can do that. I hope you like it here, gentlemen. Of course we could go somewhere else . . .

GARGA: What's the matter, Jane? Aren't you glad I've come for you?

JANE: You know perfectly well, George. And if you don't, I can't tell you.

GARGA: What do you mean?

JANE: Don't you see, George, I'm different from what you think, even if I'm almost done for. Why did you bring these gentlemen? I've always known I'd end like this.

When they told me in Sunday school what happens to the weak, I said to myself: that's what will happen to me. You don't have to prove it to anybody.

GARGA: Then you won't come home?

JANE: Don't ask me, George.

GARGA: But I am asking you, my dear.

JANE: Then I'll have to put it a different way. I've been living with this man. *Points to Baboon.* I admit it, gentlemen. And what's the use? Nothing's going to get any better.

BABOON: She's out of her mind.

MAYNES: Dreadful!

GARGA: Listen to me, Jane. This is your last chance in this city. I'm ready to wipe the slate clean. These gentlemen are my witnesses. Come home with me.

JANE: It's nice of you, George. It certainly is my last chance. But I won't take it. Things aren't right between us, you know that. I'm going now, George. *To Baboon:* Come.

BABOON: That's that. *Both go out.*

ONE OF THE MEN: That fellow has nothing to laugh about.

GARGA: I'll leave the apartment open, Jane. You can ring at night.

WORM *steps up to the table:* You've probably noticed: there's a family here in our midst, or what's left of it. Moth-eaten as it is, this family would gladly give its last cent to find out where the mother, the mainstay of the household, is keeping herself. The fact is, I saw her one morning at about seven o'clock, a woman of forty, scrubbing a fruit cellar. She's started a new business. She'd aged but she was looking all right.

GARGA: But you, sir, didn't you work in the lumber business of the man they're combing every inch of Chicago for?

WORM: Me? No, I've never laid eyes on the man. *Goes out, on his way inserting a coin in the nickelodeon. It starts playing Gounod's 'Ave Maria'.*

THE PREACHER *at a corner table reads the liquor list aloud in a hard voice, savouring each word:* Cherry Flip, Cherry Brandy, Gin Fizz, Whisky Sour, Golden Slipper, Manhattan,

Curaçao extra dry, Orange, Maraschino Cusenier, and the specialty of the house, Egg-nog. This drink is made of egg – one raw egg – sugar, cognac, Jamaica rum, milk.

THE PUGNOSED MAN: Are you familiar with those drinks, sir?

PREACHER: No!

Laughter.

GARGA *to the men with him:* It has been necessary to show you my broken family, but you can see how humiliating it is for me. You will also have realized that that yellow weed must never again be allowed to take root in our city. My sister Mary, as you know, was in Shlink's employ for some time. In speaking to her now, of course, I shall have to proceed as carefully as possible, because even in her deepest misery my sister has preserved a certain trace of delicacy. *He sits down beside Mary.* Won't you let me see your face?

MARY: It's not a face any more. It's not me.

GARGA: No. But I remember once in church – when you were nine years old – you said: let him come to me beginning to-morrow. We thought you meant God.

MARY: Did I say that?

GARGA: I still love you, soiled and wasted as you are. But even if I knew that you knew you could do as you pleased with yourself if I told you I still loved you, I'd tell you all the same.

MARY: And you can look at me when you say that? At this face?

GARGA: That face. People remain what they are even if their faces fall apart.

MARY *stands up:* But I won't have it. I don't want you to love me that way. I like myself the way I was. Don't say I was never any different.

GARGA *in a loud voice:* Do you earn money? Do you live entirely on what you get from men?

MARY: And you've brought people to hear about it? Can I have some whisky? With plenty of ice. All right, I'll tell them. All right, I threw myself away, but as soon as I'd

done it I asked for money, to make it plain what I am and
that I can live on it. It's only a business arrangement. I've
got a nice body, I never let a man smoke when he's with
me, but I'm not a virgin any more, love is my job. I've got
money here. But I'm going to earn more, I want to spend
money, it's a craving I have; when I've made money, I
don't want to save, here, I throw it down the sink. That's
the way I am.

MAYNES: Horrible!

ANOTHER MAN: You wouldn't dare to laugh.

PREACHER: Man is too durable. That's his main fault. He can
do too much to himself. He's too hard to destroy. *Goes out.*

MAYNES *standing up with the other three men:* We've seen,
Garga, that you've suffered an injustice.

THE PUGNOSED MAN *approaches Mary:* Whores! *He guffaws.*
Vice is a lady's perfume.

MARY: You call us whores. With this powder on our faces you
can't see the eyes that were blue. The men who do business
with crooks make love to us. We sell our sleep, we live on
abuse.

A shot is heard.

BARMAN: The gentleman has shot himself in the neck. *The
men bring in the Preacher and lay him down on the table among the
glasses.*

FIRST MAN: Don't touch him. Hands off.

SECOND MAN: He's trying to say something.

FIRST MAN *bending over him, in a loud voice:* Do you want anything? Have you any relatives? Where should we take you?

PREACHER *mumbles:* 'La montagne est passée: nous irons
mieux.' [11]

GARGA *standing over him, laughing:* He's missed, and in more
ways than one. He thought those were his last words, but
they're somebody else's, and anyway they're not his last
words, because his aim was bad and it's only a small flesh
wound.

FIRST MAN: So it is. Tough luck. He did it in the dark, he
should have done it in the light.

MARY: His head is hanging down. Put something under it.
How thin he is. I recognize him now. He spat in his face
one time.

All except Mary and Garga go out with the wounded man.

GARGA: His skin is too thick. It bends anything you can stick
into it. There aren't blades enough.

MARY: He's still on your mind?

GARGA: Yes, to you I can admit it.

MARY: Love and hate! How low they bring us!

GARGA: So they do. Do you still love him?

MARY: Yes . . . yes.

GARGA: And no hope of better winds?

MARY: Yes, now and then.

GARGA: I wanted to help you. *Pause.* This fight has been such
a debauch that today I need all Chicago to help me stop it.
Of course it's possible that he himself wasn't planning to go
on. He himself intimated that at his age three years can mean
as much as thirty. In view of all these circumstances I've
destroyed him with a very crude weapon. I didn't even have
to be there in person. In addition, I've made it absolutely
impossible for him to see me. This last blow will not be
discussed between us, he won't be able to find me. You
could call it a technical knockout, and on every street
corner the taxi-drivers are watching to make sure that he
won't show up in the ring again. Chicago has thrown in the
towel for him. I don't know where he is, but he knows
what's what.

BARMAN: The lumber yards in Mulberry Street are on fire.

MARY: If you've shaken him off, it's a good thing. But now
I'm going.

GARGA: I'll stay here in the middle of the lynch mob. But
I'll be home tonight. We'll live together. *Mary goes out.* Now
I'll drink black coffee again in the morning, wash my face in
cold water, and put on clean clothes, first of all a shirt. I'll
comb a good many things out of my brain in the morning;
there will be fresh noise and many things happening all
around me in the city, now that I'm rid of that passion. It

wanted to go down to the grave with me, but I've still got things to do. *Opens the door wide and listens laughing to the howling of the lynch mob that has grown louder.*

SHLINK *enters, wearing an American suit:* Are you alone? It was hard to get here. I knew you were getting out today, I've looked for you at your place. They're close at my heels. Quick, Garga, come with me.

GARGA: Are you out of your mind? I informed on you to get rid of you.

SHLINK: I'm not a brave man. I died three times on the way here.

GARGA: Yes. I hear they're hanging yellow men like linen on Milwaukee Bridge.

SHLINK: All the more reason for hurrying. You know you've got to come. We're not through yet.

GARGA *very slowly, aware of Shlink's haste:* Unfortunately your request comes at a bad time. I have company. My sister, Mary Garga, ruined in September three years ago, taken by surprise. My wife, Jane Garga, debauched at the same time. Last of all, a Salvation Army preacher, name unknown, spat on and destroyed, though it doesn't matter much. But most of all, my mother, Mae Garga, born in 1872 in the South, who disappeared three years ago this October and has vanished even from memory, now faceless. Her face fell off her like a yellow leaf. *Listens.* That howling!

SHLINK *also absorbed in listening:* Yes, but it's not the right kind of howling yet, the white kind. Then they'll be here. Then we'll still have a minute. Listen! Now! Now it's the right kind – white! Come! *Garga quickly leaves with Shlink.*

10

A Deserted Tent, formerly used by Railway Workers, in the Gravel Pits of Lake Michigan

19 November 1915, about 2 a.m.
Shlink, Garga.

SHLINK: The perpetual roar of Chicago has stopped. Seven times three days the skies have paled and the air turned grey-blue like grog. Now the silence has come, that conceals nothing.

GARGA *smoking:* Fighting comes as easy to you as digestion. I've been thinking about my childhood. The blue flax fields. The polecat in the gulches and the light-frothing rapids.

SHLINK: Right. All that was in your face. But now it's as hard as amber, which is transparent; here and there dead insects can be seen in it.

GARGA: You've always been alone?

SHLINK: Forty years.

GARGA: And now, towards the end, you've succumbed to the black plague of this planet, the lust for human contact.

SHLINK *smiling:* Through enmity?

GARGA: Through enmity.

SHLINK: Then you understand that we're comrades, comrades in a metaphysical conflict. Our acquaintance has been brief, for a time it overshadowed everything else, the time has passed quickly. The stations of life are not those of memory. The end is not the goal, the last episode is no more important than any other. Twice in my life I've owned a lumber business. For the last two weeks it has been registered in your name.

GARGA: Have you premonitions of death?

SHLINK: Here is the ledger of your lumber business; it begins where ink was once poured over the figures.

GARGA: You've been carrying it next to your skin? Open it yourself, it's sure to be filthy. *He reads.* A clean account. Nothing but withdrawals. On the seventeenth: the lumber deal. $25,000 to Garga. Just above: $10 for clothing. Below: $22 for Mary Garga, 'our' sister. At the very end: the whole business burned to the ground again. – I can't sleep any more. I'll be glad when you're covered with quicklime.

SHLINK: Don't deny the past, George! What's an account? Remember the question we raised. Brace yourself: I love you.

GARGA *looks at him:* That's disgusting! You're terrifyingly loathsome. An old man like you! [12]

SHLINK: Maybe I'll never get an answer. But if you get one, think of me when my mouth is full of dry rot. What are you listening for?

GARGA *lazily:* You show traces of feeling. You're old.

SHLINK: Is it so good to bare your teeth?

GARGA: If they're good teeth.

SHLINK: Man's infinite isolation makes enmity an unattainable goal. But even with the animals understanding is not possible.

GARGA: Speech isn't enough to create understanding.

SHLINK: I've observed the animals. Love, the warmth of bodies in contact, is the only mercy shown us in the darkness. But the only union is that of the organs, and it can't bridge over the cleavage made by speech. Yet they unite in order to produce beings to stand by them in their hopeless isolation. And the generations look coldly into each other's eyes. If you cram a ship full to bursting with human bodies, they'll all freeze with loneliness. Are you listening, Garga? Yes, so great is man's isolation that not even a fight is possible. The forest! That's where mankind comes from. Hairy, with apes' jaws, good animals who knew how to live. Everything was so easy. They simply tore each other apart. I see them clearly, with quivering flanks, staring into the whites of each other's eyes, sinking their teeth into each other's throats and rolling down. And the one who bled to death among the roots was the vanquished, and the one who had trampled down the most undergrowth was the victor. Are you listening for something, Garga?[13]

GARGA: Shlink, I've been listening to you now for three weeks. I've been waiting the whole time for a rage to take hold of me, under any pretext, however slight. But now, looking at you, I realize that your drivel irritates me and your voice sickens me.[14] Isn't this Thursday night? How far is it to New York? Why am I sitting here wasting my time? Haven't we been lying around here for three weeks now? We thought the planet would change its course on our account. But what happened? Three times it rained, and one night the wind blew. *Stands up.* Shlink, I think the time has come for you to take off your shoes. Take your shoes off, Shlink, and let me have them. Because I doubt if you've got much money left. Shlink, here in the woods of Lake Michigan I'm putting an end to our fight now going into its fourth year, because its substance is used up: it's ending right now. I can't finish it off with a knife, I see no need for high-sounding words. My shoes are full of holes and your speeches don't keep my toes warm. It's the old story, Shlink: the younger man wins.

SHLINK: Today we've heard the shovels of the railroad workers from time to time. I saw you pricking up your ears. You're standing up, Garga? You're going there, Garga? You're going to betray me?

GARGA *lying down lazily:* Yes, Shlink, that's exactly what I'm going to do.

SHLINK: And there will never be an outcome to this fight, George Garga? Never an understanding?

GARGA: No.

SHLINK: But you'll come out of it with nothing to show but your bare life.

GARGA: Bare life is better than any other kind of life.

SHLINK: Tahiti?

GARGA: New York. *Laughing ironically:* 'I will go and I will return with iron limbs and dark skin, with fury in my eyes. My face will make people think that I come of a strong race. I will have gold, I will be lazy and brutal. Women love to nurse wild, sick men, returned from the hot countries. I will swim, trample grass, hunt, and most of all smoke. And down drinks as hot as boiling metal. I will mingle with life and be saved.'[15] – What nonsense! Words on a planet that's not in the centre. Long after lime has covered you through the natural elimination of the obsolete, I shall be choosing the things that amuse me.

SHLINK: What kind of an attitude is that? Kindly take your pipe out of your filthy mouth. If you're trying to tell me you've gone impotent, take a different tone at least.

GARGA: Whatever you say.

SHLINK: That gesture shows me you're unworthy to be my opponent.

GARGA: I was only deploring the fact that you bored me.

SHLINK: What's that? You deploring? You! A hired pug! A drunken salesman! Whom I bought for ten dollars, an idealist who couldn't tell his two legs apart, a nobody!

GARGA *laughing:* A young man! Be frank.

SHLINK: A white man, hired to drag me down, to stuff my mouth with disgust or dry rot, to give me the taste of death on my tongue. Six hundred feet away in the woods I'll find all the men I need to lynch me.

GARGA: Yes, maybe I'm a leper, but what of it? You're a suicide. What more have you to offer me? You hired me, but you never paid up.

SHLINK: You got what a man like you needs. I bought you furniture.

GARGA: Yes, I got a piano out of you, a piano that had to be sold. I ate meat *once*. I bought one suit, and for your idiotic talk I gave up my sleep.

SHLINK: Your sleep, your mother, your sister and your wife. Three years off your stupid life. But how annoying! It's all ending in banality. You never understood what it was all about. You wanted me dead. But I wanted a fight. Not of the flesh but of the spirit.

GARGA: And the spirit, you see, is nothing. The important thing is not to be stronger, but to come off alive. I can't defeat you, I can only stamp you into the ground. I'll carry my raw flesh into the icy rains, Chicago is cold. I'm going there now. Possibly I'm doing the wrong thing. But I have plenty of time. *Goes out.*

Shlink falls down.

SHLINK *standing up:* Now that the last sword thrusts have been exchanged as well as the last words that occurred to us, I thank you for the interest you have shown in my person. A good deal has fallen away from us, we have hardly more than our naked bodies left. In four minutes the moon will rise, then your lynch mob will be here. *He notices that Garga has gone and follows him.* Don't go, George Garga! Don't quit because you're young. The forests have been cut down, the vultures are glutted, and the golden answer will be buried deep in the ground. *Turns. A milky light is seen in the brush.* November nineteenth. Three miles south of Chicago. West wind. Four minutes before the rising of the moon, drowned while fishing.

MARY *enters:* Please don't drive me away. I'm an unhappy woman.

The light grows stronger in the brush.

SHLINK: It's all piling up. Fish swimming into your mouth ... What's that crazy light? I'm very busy.

MARY *removing her hat:* I'm not pretty any more. Don't look at me. The rats have gnawed at me. I'm bringing you what's left.

SHLINK: That strange milky light! Ah, that's it! Phosphorescent rot, that's it!

MARY: Does my face look bloated to you?

SHLINK: Do you realize you'll be lynched if the mob catches you here?

MARY: It's all the same to me.

SHLINK: I beg you, leave me alone in my last moments.

MARY: Come. Hide in the underbrush. There's a hiding-place in the quarry.

SHLINK: Damn it! Are you out of your mind? Don't you see that I have to cast one last look over this jungle? That's what the moon is rising for. *Steps into the entrance of the tent.*

MARY: All I see is that you've lost the ground from under your feet. Have pity on yourself.

SHLINK: Can't you do me this one last kindness?

MARY: I only want to look at you. I've found out that this is where I belong.

SHLINK: Maybe so! Then stay. *A signal is heard in the distance.* Two o'clock. I've got to find safety.

MARY: Where's George?

SHLINK: George? He's run away. What a miscalculation! Safety. *He tears off his scarf.* The barrels are beginning to stink. Good fat fish, I caught them myself. Well-dried, packed up in crates. Salted. First set out in ponds, bought, overpaid, fattened! Fish eager for death, suicidal fish, that swallow hooks like holy wafers. Phoo! Quick now! *He goes to the table, sits down. Drinks from a flask.* I, Wang Yeng, known as Shlink, born in Yokohama in northern Peiho under the sign of the Tortoise. I operated a lumber business, ate rice, and dealt with all sorts of people. I, Wang Yeng, known as Shlink, aged fifty-four, ended three miles south of Chicago without heirs.

MARY: What's the matter?

SHLINK *seated:* You here? My legs are getting cold. Throw a cloth over my face. Have pity. *He collapses.*
Panting in the underbrush. Footsteps and hoarse curses from behind.

MARY: What are you listening for? Answer me. Are you asleep? Are you still cold? I'm here, close to you. What did you want with the cloth?
At this moment knives cut openings in the tent. The lynchers step silently through the openings.

MARY *going towards them:* Go away. He just died. He doesn't want anyone to look at him.

11

The Private Office of the late C. Shlink

A week later
*The lumber yard has burned down. Signs here and there saying:
'Business for Sale'. Garga, John Garga, Mary Garga.*

JOHN: It was stupid of you to let this place burn down. Now
all you've got is charred beams. Who's going to buy them?

GARGA *laughing:* They're cheap. But what are you two planning to do?

JOHN: I thought we'd stay together.

GARGA *laughing:* I'm leaving. Are you going to work?

MARY: I'm going to work. But not scrub stairs like my
mother.[16]

JOHN: I'm a soldier. We slept in watering troughs. The rats
on our faces never weighed less than seven pounds. When
they took away my rifle and it was over, I said: From now
on we'll all sleep with our caps on.

GARGA: You mean: we'll all sleep.

MARY: We'd better go now, Father. Night's coming on, and
I still have no room.

JOHN: Yes, let's go. *Looks around.* Let's go. A soldier at your
side. Forward march! Against the jungle of the city.

GARGA: I've got it behind me. Hello!

MANKY *comes in beaming, with his hands in his pockets:* It's me. I
read your ad in the paper. If your lumber business doesn't
cost too much, I'll buy it.

GARGA: What's your offer?

MANKY: Why are you selling?

GARGA: I'm going to New York.

MANKY: And I'm moving in here.

GARGA: How much can you pay?

MANKY: I'll need some cash for the business.

GARGA: Six thousand, if you'll take the woman too.

MANKY: All right.

MARY: I've got my father with me.

MANKY: And your mother?

MARY: She's not here any more.

MANKY *after a pause:* All right.

MARY: Draw up the contract.

The men sign.

MANKY: Let's all have a bite. Want to come along, George?

GARGA: No.

MANKY: Will you still be here when we get back?

GARGA: No.

JOHN: Good-bye, George. Take a look at New York. You can come back to Chicago if the going gets too rough.

The three go out.

GARGA *putting the money away:* It's a good thing to be alone. The chaos is spent. That was the best time.

Notes and Variants

TEXTS BY BRECHT

THREE EARLY NOTES

(1) The play is set in an unreal, chilly Chicago. Shlink wears a long dirty yellow costume down to his ankles, picturesquely blackened hair, and a black tuft on his chin.

George Garga is like A. Rimbaud in appearance. He is essentially a German translation into American from the French.

(2) Towards the end of *Jungle*

Everything performed in front of a cyclorama. At the back all the actors not immediately involved sit in a dusty light, following the script. When Jane Garga dies she drops hers, and so on.

(3) A play

Chicago

The timber dealer Shlink, a Malay (Wegener's type), fights a war of annihilation with the younger George Garga (Granach's type), during the course of which both reveal their most extreme human characteristics. By means of an appearance of passivity the man Shlink slashes through the ties binding young George Garga to the world round him and makes him fight a desperate war of liberation against the steadily thickening jungle of Shlink's intrigues against him. Shlink's timber business and Garga's family are among those annihilated. Increasingly isolated, more and more tightly entangled, the two go into the woods to fight it out. In the final conflict, which is fought with utter dedication, George Garga regains solid ground; he breaks off the fight (which was the man Shlink's final sensation) and takes over his timber business in the great city of Chicago.

The events dealt with are concrete ones; the fight for the timber business, the family, a marriage, the fight for personal freedom. There are not many characters, no walking-on parts.

[From Bertolt Brecht: *Im Dickicht der Städte*. Erstfassung und Materialien. Edited by Gisela E. Bahr. Suhrkamp, Frankfurt, 1968, pp. 134, 136–7. Paul Wegener and Alexander Granach were prominent German actors of the time.]

PROGRAMME NOTE TO THE 1922 TEXT

The judicial proceedings to clarify the *Jane Garga murder mystery* led to the unmasking of one of those *sinister affairs in Chinatown* in Chicago which are so irresponsibly exploited by the press. A *Malayan timber merchant's fishing expedition* in a lending library, the almost total *ruination* of an immigrant *family* of French descent, the *mysterious lynching of the Malay*.

The play before you provides a possibly somewhat rough piece of theatrical carpentry whose raw material would certainly interest a wider public. There are a fair number of gaps in it. It omits even points which the proceedings cleared up, such as the *Malayan murderer's crimes*, thanks to which he regained possession of his *timber business donated to the Salvation Army*, and which characterized his flight into the yellow swamps with George Garga as an act of fear of the *lynch law of the respectable population*. Others remained obscure, and will no doubt always remain so. The *fate of Mae Garga*, her whereabouts, her motives for abandoning a family she had cared for for many years, have never been cleared up.

The present stage text is primarily intended to make theatrical material of *certain remarkable incidents* whose originals in real life appear to have taken place in the gloomy September of 1914 in *Chicago's Chinatown*, and whose consequences will no doubt be recalled from the newspapers. Accordingly only extracts are given of the few conversations that concern us here (for this unusual and most horrific story reposes only on a small number of conversations, whose substance was difficult and expensive to get at). They consist, making allowance for some clarifications and *improbabilities* such as are *inevitable* to the drama and for a perhaps over-*romantic embroidery* of the events due to stage requirements, simply in the most important sentences uttered here at a specific point on the globe's surface at specific moments in *the history of mankind.*

[Ibid., pp. 9–10. Brecht instructed that the italicized words should be shouted from behind the curtain before the start of the play, in imitation of newspaper sellers' cries.]

SYNOPSIS (*incomplete*)

i. A Malay called C. Shlink appears in the life of George Garga and for no known reason starts a fight. He tries Garga out to establish his fighting qualities, then starts by annihilating his economic existence.

ii. George Garga fights back.

iii. Shlink gives up his property so as to fight on equal terms. He thereby arouses the interest of Marie Garga, his enemy's sister.

iv. Garga abandons his family so as not to be hampered in the fight. Shlink moves into the vacant space.

v. Garga has vanished. Shlink has summoned up his reserves.

vi. Garga reappears, determined to exploit Shlink's fighting mood to further his own and his sister's objectives.

vii. Shlink is ready to follow out Garga's instructions.

viii. Garga tries to dig in behind his family. This results in the Garga family's total liquidation. Garga himself disappears provisionally into prison, but not unprovided with weapons.

[Ibid., p. 137, with the suggested date 1923–4.]

A STATEMENT

At one or two points in my play *Jungle* a character quotes verses by Rimbaud and Verlaine. In the script these passages are marked as quotations by means of inverted commas. Apparently the stage has no technique by which to express quotation marks. If it had, then a considerable number of other favourite works would become possibly more palatable for literary scholars but pretty intolerable for the audience. In view of the difficulty of their craft, those currently concerned with the manufacture of plays are unlikely, I fear, to have time either now or in the next ten years to sit back and think about such matters. Interested parties from the world of scholarship are accordingly invited to ring back in eleven years or so. (It can be divulged here and now that if the drama is to progress at all it will progress surely and serenely over the dead bodies of the scholars.)

['Eine Feststellung', from GW *Schriften zum Theater*, p. 969. This appeared in the *Berliner Börsen-Courier* of 4 November 1924, after an article by Herwarth Walden in *Die Republik* of 31 October complaining of Brecht's borrowings. There were statements under the same heading by the Rimbaud translator Hans Jacob, siding with Walden, and by Herbert Ihering, pooh-poohing such revelations.]

PROLOGUE TO 'JUNGLE'

What was new was a type of man who conducted a fight without enmity but with hitherto unheard of (i.e. undepicted) methods, together with his attitude to the family, to marriage, to his fellow-humans in general, and much else – probably too much. That wasn't, however, what people regard as new. The sort of thing they regard as new is the machine, in other words something they can use without having made it or being able to understand it. In literature the last thing to strike them as new is the idea, say, that a husband ought not to treat his wife as a doll, or that marriage is dangerous, or that a cart-driver can be just as tragic as a more highly placed individual, indeed more so in that he doesn't know his way around so well.

To those with this culinary outlook, formal novelty lies

exclusively in the packaging. Since we were served up in the oldest possible packaging we were not new enough. 'Valencia' with jazz is new. It's not particularly new without. Jazz itself is of course new.

['Neu und alt' from GW *Schriften zum Theater*, p. 67. ?About 1926.]

PROGRAMME NOTE FOR THE HEIDELBERG PRODUCTION

Visiting the play *In the Jungle of Cities* has turned out to be such a difficult proposition that only the most courageous theatres have been prepared to tackle it. Indeed nobody should be surprised if the audience rejects the play entirely. The play rests on certain assumptions, which is always troublesome, which is why the general run of the drama avoids it. The following notes about these assumptions will be of little or no help.

2

The behaviour of our contemporaries, as frequently though by no means fully expressed in the newspapers, is no longer to be explained by old motives (largely borrowed from literature). An increasing number of police reports attribute no 'motive' to the criminal. That being so, it ought not to surprise you if the newer plays show certain types of person in certain situations behaving differently from what you expected, or if your guesses as to the motives for a particular piece of behaviour turn out to be wrong. *This is a world, and a kind of drama, where the philosopher can pick his way better than the psychologist.*

3

In the theatre as elsewhere, the bourgeoisie, having wasted a hundred years staging fights between men merely over women, is not going to have much time left for fights over more serious matters before it finds itself forced, in the theatre as elsewhere, to concentrate on the most serious of all contemporary fights, the class struggle. An idealized fight such as can be seen in the play *In the Jungle of Cities* is at present only to be found in the theatre. For the real thing you will have to wait fifty years.

4

In the meantime I am sure you see that I still need to defend the simple basic conception of the play *In the Jungle of Cities*. This is that pure sport might involve two men in a fight which transforms them and their economic circumstances to the point of unrecognizability. The passion for sport is here being classed with all the other passions already at the theatre's disposal. No doubt it will take at least five decades of continuous practice in at least two continents before this passion is put on an emotional par with those great and tragic passions liable to produce triumphs and catastrophes on the grand scale. What I mean is: there are catastrophes today whose motive is sport even though it cannot be recognized as such. Besides this continuous practice there will have to be an end to those other, less pure motives for fighting which still preponderate, such as the urge to own women or means of production or objects of exploitation: motives, in short, that *can* come to an end since they can simply be organized away.

5

The territory used for fighting in this play is probably unfamiliar. For the territory so used consists in certain complexes of ideas such as a young man like George Garga holds about the family, about marriage or about his own honour. His opponent uses these complexes of ideas in order to damage him. Moreover, each combatant stimulates such thoughts in the other as must destroy him; he shoots burning arrows into his head. I can't explain this way of fighting more clearly than that.

6

My choice of an American setting is not, as has frequently been suggested, the result of a romantic disposition. I could just as well have picked Berlin, except that then the audience, instead of saying, 'That character's acting strangely, strikingly, peculiarly,' would simply have said 'It's a very exceptional Berliner who behaves like that.' Using a background (American) which naturally suited my characters, covering them rather than showing them up, seemed the easiest way of drawing attention to the odd behaviour of widely representative contemporary human types. In a German setting these same types would have been romantic; they would have contrasted with their setting, not with a romantic audience. In practical terms I would be satisfied if theatres projected America photographically on the backcloth and were content to imply Shlink's Asiatic origin by means of a plain yellow make-up, generally allowing him to behave like an Asiatic, in other words like a European. That would keep at least *one* major mystery out of the play.

['Für das Programmheft der Heidelberger Aufführung',
24 July 1928, from GW *Schriften zum Theater*, p. 969.]

ON LOOKING THROUGH MY FIRST PLAYS (iii)

My memories of writing the play *In the Jungle of Cities* are far from clear, but at least I remember the desires and ideas with which I was seized. One factor was my having seen a production of Schiller's *The Robbers*: one of those bad performances whose very poverty emphasizes the outlines of a good play, so that the writer's high aims are brought out by the failure to fulfil them. In *The Robbers* there is a most furious, destructive and desperate fight over a bourgeois inheritance, using partly non-bourgeois means. What interested me about this fight was its fury, and because it was a time (the early 1920s) when I appreciated sport, and boxing in particular, as one of the 'great mythical diversions of the giant cities on the other side

of the herring pond' I wanted my new play to show the con-
clusion of a 'fight for fighting's sake', a fight with no origin
other than the pleasure of fighting and no object except to
decide who is 'the best man'. I ought to add that at that time I
had in mind a strange historical conception, a history of mankind seen through incidents on the mass scale and of specific
historical significance, a history of continually new and different modes of behaviour, observable here and there on our
planet.

My play was meant to deal with this pure enjoyment of
fighting. Even while working on the first draft I noticed how
singularly difficult it was to bring about a meaningful fight –
which meant, according to the views which I then held, a
fight that proved something – and keep it going. Gradually it
turned into a play about the difficulty of bringing such a
fight about. The main characters had recourse to one measure
after another in their effort to come to grips. As their battle-
ground they chose the family of one of the fighters, his place
of work, and so on and so forth. The other fighter's property
was likewise 'thrown in' – and with that I was unconsciously
moving very close to the real struggle which was then taking
place, though only idealized by me: the class struggle. In the
end it dawned on the fighters that their fight was mere
shadow-boxing; even as enemies they could not make contact. A vague realization emerged: that under advanced
capitalism fighting for fighting's sake is only a wild distortion
of competition for competition's sake. The play's dialectic is
of a purely idealistic kind.

At the same time one or two seemingly quite formal wishes
were involved. In Berlin I had seen Jessner's production of
Othello with Fritz Kortner and Hofer at the then State
Theatre on the Gendarmenmarkt, and had been impressed by
one of its technical aspects: the lighting. Jessner had used
intersecting spotlights to create a peculiar dusty light which
strongly emphasized the figures; they moved about in it like
figures by Rembrandt. Other impressions also played a part:
my reading of Rimbaud's *Une saison en enfer* and of J. V. Jen-

sen's Chicago novel *The Wheel*. Also the reading of a collection
of letters whose name I forget; they had a chilly, conclusive
tone almost like that of a will. The influence of the outskirts
of Augsburg should also be mentioned. I often used to go to
the annual autumn *Plärrer*, a fair with sideshows on the so-
called Small Parade Ground, with music from a number of
roundabouts and with panoramas showing such naïve art as
'The Shooting of the Anarchist Ferrer in Madrid' or 'Nero
Watching while Rome Burns' or 'The Lions of Bavaria
Storming the Earthworks at Düppel' or 'Flight of Charles the
Bold after the Battle of Murten'. I remember Charles the
Bold's horse. He had huge scared eyes, as if aware of the
historical situation. I wrote the play very largely out of doors
while walking. An alley of Spanish chestnuts ran parallel with
the old city moat past my father's house; beyond it were the
wall and the remnants of the fortifications. The chestnuts
were shedding their yellow leaves. The paper I wrote on was
thin typing paper, folded in four to fit inside my leather note-
book. I made concoctions of words like strong drinks, entire
scenes out of words whose texture and colour were specific-
ally designed to make an impression on the senses. Cherry-
stone, revolver, trouserpocket, paper god: concoctions of that
kind. At the same time I was of course working on the story,
on the characters, on my views of human conduct and its
effectiveness. I may be slightly overstressing the formal side,
but I wanted to show what a complex business such writing is
and how one thing merges into the other: how the shape
arises from the material and in turn moulds it. Both before
and later I worked in a different way and on different prin-
ciples, and the resulting plays were simpler and more materialistic, but there too a considerable formal element was
absorbed by the material as they took shape.

[From 'Bei Durchsicht meiner ersten Stücke' in GW *Schriften
zum Theater*, pp. 949–50. Dated March 1954. Brecht reviewed a
production of *The Robbers* at the Augsburg municipal theatre on
23 October 1920. Leopold Jessner's Berlin production of
Othello with Fritz Kortner, Johanna Hofer, Albert Steinrück

and Rudolf Forster had its première on 11 November 1921;
it must have been one of the first plays that he saw in Berlin. For
a note on Brecht's debt to Rimbaud and Jensen, see p. 450
below. The collection of letters, so Dr Reinhold Grimm has
suggested, may be a volume called *Knabenbriefe* edited by
Charlotte Westermann and published in Düsseldorf in 1908.]

Editorial Note on the Text

This is based, with grateful acknowledgements, on the texts and information given in the volume of 'materials' edited by Gisela E. Bahr under the title *Im Dickicht der Städte. Erstfassung und Materialien*, and published by Suhrkamp-Verlag in 1968 ('edition suhrkamp' number 246). References in the text are to the notes on The Play's Literary Ancestry, which follow on p. 84.

A diary note of 11 September 1921 shows Brecht just before his visit to Berlin wondering why 'nobody has yet described the big city as a jungle'.

> Where are its heroes, its colonisers, its victims? The hostility of the big city, its malignant stony consistency, its babylonian confusion of language: in short, its poetry has not yet been created.

As he was then fresh from reading Jensen's *The Wheel* and Sinclair's *The Jungle*, both of which are set in Chicago, this cannot be taken too literally, but it relates none the less to the first draft of the play, on which he embarked about that time.

In the Jungle, as it was then called, had its première on 9 May 1923. The typescript (of which two versions exist in the Brecht Archive) had by then already been considerably modified, to judge from the evidence of the two heavily amended scripts used by the director Erich Engel (and left by him to the East German Academy of Arts) and of the printed programme. Thus there are sixteen scenes in the typescript, but the programme says it is a 'Drama in 10 Scenes'. It evidently began with the shouted headlines from the Programme Note (p. 66 above), and lasted over three hours. At the first Berlin performance, which took place on 29 October 1924 at the Deutsches Theater, again under Engel's direction, it was renamed *Jungle*, with the subtitle 'Decline of a Family' and prefaced by the present prologue. Essentially, however, it seems to have been a cut version of the same play.

The revised *In the Jungle of Cities*, virtually in its final form, was published by Ullstein (Propyläen-Verlag) in spring 1927, and given its first performance under Carl Ebert's direction in Darmstadt that

December. There are eleven scenes (though misnumbering makes it look as if there were only ten); their titles have been made apparently more precise, with exact dates and times; stage and lighting directions are less atmospheric; some names and characters are altered, notably those of Skinny and Manky; there are fewer references to the jungle and more to the fight; a generally more urban, American, technological flavour is given, not least by the illustrations at the end of the book, which show 'typical cities and people of the first decades of the century'. There are also some major alterations in the story: Jane's murder is dispensed with; the illegal reselling of Shlink's timber is new, and the lynchers who come for him in the end are no longer individuals he has wronged but citizens responding to a denunciation made by Garga before he goes to gaol and left smouldering under Shlink like a kind of time-bomb.

In the 1950s a few very small changes were made when the play was republished in Brecht's collected *Stücke*. Among them are the substitution of 'Schönes' (or 'beautiful') for Manky's odd English term of endearment 'Nice', and the cutting of the dedication to Brecht's first wife Marianne.

The following is a scene by scene comparison of the typescript (corrected version) of *In the Jungle* (1922) and the published text of *In the Jungle of Cities* (1927). Arabic scene numbers refer to the former, Roman to the latter.

1. *Lending Library.* (Fairly close to I.)

Described as '*Brown. Wet tobacco leaves. Soapy-green sliding windows, steps. Low. Lots of paper*'. Shlink (who had originally been conceived of as Chinese) wears a '*long dirty yellow soutane*'. According to Engel's script he 'speaks quickly, but with large slow gestures, never giving anything away. Broad, powerful back.' Moti Gui, who was renamed Skinny in the 1927 text, 'has a rather asthmatic snuffle. Rhythmic speech due to pauses for breath. Half-breed, run down, agog for sensations.' Worm, who then had no other name, is 'bald, syphilitic. Saddle-shaped nose, wide-set eyes. Genial.' Baboon, likewise, 'A pimp. Dressed in greasy black. Occasionally imitates Shlink.'

The references to Jensen and Rimbaud early in the scene are new in 1927. In 1922 Garga at one point recommends 'Noa! Noa! A good, first rate book, written in blood on leather ...' and Brecht evidently considered inserting a quotation from this work of Gauguin's to follow Shlink's first reference to Tahiti.

By 1927 pounds had become dollars and schnaps whisky. Garga's references to prostitution and Shlink's declaration that he is opening the fight against him and will shake his foundations are all new.

2. *In the Quarry*. (Cut.)

This dialogue between Garga and The Green Man is given in full at the end of the present notes. It was cut from the 1927 version, and probably also from the two earlier productions as, although it is in Engel's and Erwin Faber's (the Munich Garga)'s scripts, The Green Man is not named on the 1923 programme.

3. *Shlink's office*. (Cut and slightly transposed to form II.)

Described as 'Brown, like an open sluice-gate'. In lieu of the opening exchange with Worm, Shlink soliloquizes:

> Smooth, round, full, that's me. It's all so little effort, it all comes easy to me. How easily I digest! *Silence*. For ten years there's been no difficulty in living like this. Comfortable, well dug in, avoiding any kind of friction. Now I've begun to take easiness for granted, and I'm fed up with everything.

Marie enters in white. As Garga puts on his new linen behind the screen he exclaims 'White linen! That means adventures. White muslin. For daydreaming about horses in.' He makes his remark about Shlink having stripped his skin (now on p. 12) immediately after emerging from behind the screen, thus establishing the relation between the two leit-motivs of *skin* and *linen*.

The resale of Broost and Co's timber is all new in 1927. In the 1922 text the sacking of Moti Gui (= Skinny) is more elaborate. Baboon is not in this scene at all (nor are his remarks re Papua and 'the chick'), so when Shlink tells Marie 'he loves you' he is referring to Moti Gui – altogether a more pathetic and less comic character in this version. He tries to woo Marie by telling her that she gives off a smell like a horse; hence Garga's remark at the end of the scene, which remains, a little bafflingly, in the 1927 text. In a sub-episode labelled 'The Auction' and cut in the second of Engel's scripts Marie is inspected 'like a horse' and has been put up for auction when the Salvation Army arrive. Her closing lines to the scene are new.

4. *The Family Sacrificed*. (III is much the same, but plus the episode with Worm and subsequent references to it.)

The setting is an '*attic with light-coloured wallpaper. Ivory people.*

Dark circular table. John, Mae, Mankyboddle seated around it.' Mankyboddle, sometimes called Manky for short in this version, is
altogether more prominent and more emphatically an old sea dog
than in 1927. A very early note referring to Marie's suitor as
'(Kutteldaddeldu)' suggests that both name and character may
derive from Joachim Ringelnatz's comic seaman of that name.

More is made in 1922 of the tension between the Garga parents,
also of George Garga's drinking. 'This is a city,' says John before
George's entrance, 'people live in holes like this; my brother ran
around in the jungle – the deserter. George has got his blood.' It is
new in 1927 that George should bring money and hand it to Mae.
The episode with Worm is already in two of the 1923 stage scripts.

In one of these when John and Manky reappear before Shlink's
entrance they sing a verse of the 'Ballad of the Woman and the
Soldier' (subsequently used in *Mother Courage*). In the other they
sing 'Fifteen men on the dead man's chest' from *Treasure Island*.
It is suggested that they did so in the Munich production.

5. *In the Coal Yards.* (Replaced by IV 'Chinese Hotel', which was
evidently written for the 1923 production.)

In the first half Marie, who has been bringing food to Shlink as
he heaves coal, declares her love for him and is rejected. The second
is a long battle of words between him and Garga, ending with the
latter's refusal to go to Tahiti. In the background 'the thunder of
awakening Chicago'.

The 1923 'Chinese Hotel' scene is largely the same as in the 1927
text, the chief addition in the latter being Baboon's opening
remarks about Shlink's activities.

6. *In the Sack.* (Cut and partly rewritten to form V, the second
Chinese Hotel scene.)

'Schnaps saloon in the Coal Bar. Divided by sacking, though
not completely.' The division is in effect as in V. Garga is lying on
the bed 'psalmodizing'; Manky is sitting drinking in the saloon.
There are even more Rimbaud quotations or imitations than in
1927, and an introductory episode where Worm and Moti Gui/
Skinny report to Garga, and the latter humiliates Moti Gui by
throwing a coin into the washing-up water and getting him to fish
it out with his teeth. In the 1927 text Skinny is not in this scene.

Marie and Garga have more to say about their parents' plight.
Shlink announces that he has bought back his house. Garga tells
Shlink that he is beginning to feel at home in his skin; then when

he tries to cadge a drink Shlink says he can't buy his skin with money. The general gist of the scene remains the same, though it is new in 1927 that Shlink should hand over the proceeds of the Broost timber sale and then be treated as 'overdrawn'.

7. *Mankyboddle's Attic.* (Cut from 1927 text.)

'*Greenish wallpaper.*' A short scene between Manky and Marie. Her desperate efforts to love him have been too much for both. She denounces him and goes out, leaving him muttering, 'Nice! Christ, what a hysterical cow you are! Nice!'

Manky is rum-sodden and nautical in this scene. Thus:

MARIE: You puff away at your cigar and lie in bed with your clothes on. Why don't you take your pants off?
MANKY: I got the habit on the *Anaqueen*, see?

The scene is in Engel's script, but has evidently not been worked on and is deleted from the list of scenes there.

8. *At the Gargas'.* (Telescoped with scene 10 to form VII.)

'*Attic. Sacking. Whitewash. Circular table. Midday meal.*' About five-sixths of the scene are cut in the 1927 version, and there is a good deal of cutting already in the 1923 stage scripts. About a third of scene 10 (q.v.) is tacked on to what remains.

The evidence of prosperity in the Gargas' room – the new clothes and furniture and John's opening speech – is absent from the 1922 version, which begins with a desultory mealtime conversation in which Manky is prominent. He also plays the accordion, and later joins John in singing verses taken (unacknowledgedly) from Kipling's *The Light That Failed*:

There were three friends that buried the fourth,
The mould in his mouth and the dust in his eyes,
And they went south and east and north –
The strong man fights but the sick man dies.

There were three friends that spoke of the dead –
The strong man fights and the sick man dies –
'And would he were here with us now,' they said –
'The sun in our face and the wind in our eyes.'

In 1927 Manky is named in the opening stage direction, but has nothing to say.

Between Shlink's entry and Jane's description of the wedding about 130 lines are cut. Shlink announces that Marie has left

Manky, then the landlord appears demanding the rent and complaining of the accordion. Shlink produces the title deeds to some
southern cotton fields and hands them to Garga, thus saving the
family. A reference by Garga to the 'chalky light' is changed in
1927 to 'a cold light'.

The mention of the Broost timber swindle and of Garga's
intention to go to gaol is new in 1927. The scene ends with Mae's
disappearance and the entry of the waiter with John's farewell
drink.

9. *Coppice*. (VI.)

'*Low trees with faded brown leaves. Whiteish mist.*' Taken over almost
unchanged in 1927, but transposed to precede the foregoing
scene. The word 'jungle' is used instead of 'bushes' where Shlink
speaks of Marie being like a [crazy] bitch.

10. *Garga's Attic*. (Telescoped with 8 to form VII.)

'*Yellow wallpaper. Watercolour. Evening drips down the panes like
dishwater.*' Most of the rest of VII after the waiter's exit is from the
beginning of this scene: i.e. Marie's attempt to give John Garga
money. Garga's reappearance, however, and his writing of the
note to the newspaper (the police in 1927) are new.

In 1922 Shlink arrives after Marie's exit, and accuses Garga of
raising money in a bar on his cottonfield deeds. In fact Jane was
responsible, but Garga is prepared to take the blame and go to
prison. He threatens Shlink with a knife; Shlink challenges him to
plunge it into his breast.

11. *Bar*. (Transposed and cut to form IX.)

Scene VIII in the 1927 text is entirely new. IX, called 'Bar in
Chinatown' in 1927, was rechristened, as we now have it, in the
1953 *Stücke* volume. In 1922 the setting is not described. The
characters named include The Yellow Gentleman (not listed in the
1923 programme) – he tells the G. Wishu story – and Moti Gui
(Skinny). Worm is not in this scene.

After the Wishu story the Snub-nosed Man asks, 'Do you believe
in God?'

> THE YELLOW GENTLEMAN: No. By no means. Not in any
> sense. Absolutely not. I'm an anti-semite.

Otherwise, apart from the absence of Baboon's opening remarks
(new in 1927), the beginning of the scene up to Garga's entrance is

much as in the final version. Garga, however, appears alone, without witnesses. The arrangement of his dialogues with Jane and with Marie is rather different, though their substance is much the same. Jane, on going off with Baboon, leaves the possibility of returning to Garga open. The Salvation Army man's attempted suicide is put at the end of the scene.

Garga's speech about the fight, the ring and the knock-out is new in 1927. Shlink's entrance at the end of IX is taken over in very shortened form from scene 12 below.

12. *Garga's Attic.* (A few lines taken into IX; otherwise cut.)
   '*Night. Flying shouts from below. The partition seems to be rocking. A ship.*' Three-quarters of the scene is Shlink and Garga. Garga looks out of the window and sees 'Black linen hanging on the balcony. No wind.' Shlink thinks the shouting is getting louder.

> GARGA: They're looking for you. *Silence.* They're going to lynch us. They might . . . They might lynch us. They've been lynching today. Niggers strung up like like dirty linen. I heard on the Milwaukee Bridge that they were looking for you, – you.

Shlink again calls it 'the white howling'. (*His* lynching party, however, is only organized in scene 14.)

They leave together to go 'down to the marshes'. Then Jane and Baboon appear and occupy the rest of the scene. She is drunk, and he makes her write a note to Garga saying she is coming to him.

13. *In the Jungle.* (Telescoped with scenes 14 and 15, with a good deal of transposition, to form X.)
   '*Brown. Golden.*' The scene is confined to Shlink and Garga, who begin by speaking of their enmity, somewhat as at the start of X but at greater length. Shlink then gives Garga Jane's note.
   In Engel's stage scripts the scene is cut and partly incorporated in 15.

14. *Bar in the Jungle.* (Almost entirely cut.)
   No description of setting. Characters are The Bear, The Chair, The Ape, The Preacher, joined shortly by Garga and Moti Gui. The first three are not listed in the 1923 programme, but the stage scripts suggests that Chair and Ape are identical with Worm and Baboon.
   Bear reads in his paper that a woman's body has been found in

the marshes. Garga on entering speaks of his enmity with the Malay. Asked if it is a business matter he says, 'A physical affair. You must help me, because we've all been moulded from the same earth. Is this our country or not?'

THE OTHERS: It's our country! He shall hang! They're our trees!

Garga works them up into a lynching party. 'Are you free?' he calls after them. 'Come down into the dark arena. Your knife in your hand, bare in the cold blackness. . . . Are you free? Your mistress, freedom, is sailing on the ships!'

15. *Hut in the Jungle.* (See 13. Most of X derives from this scene.)
   Again Shlink and Garga talking about their fight. 'Yes,' says Shlink. 'You wanted it to end, but I wanted a fight, Garga.' He offers to lend him a horse to escape on. Then shows him the books of the timber business, where Garga finds as the final entry: 'Twenty pounds for strangling Jane Garga in the yellow swamps.' Garga's speech on p. 173 beginning 'Shlink, I've been listening to you now for three weeks' is new in the 1927 edition, which also adds Garga's 'New York' after Shlink's 'Tahiti?', thus altering the direction of Garga's Rimbaud quotation. The words 'in the eyes of God' are cut where Garga, just before his exit, says that it is not important to be the stronger man.
   Marie enters in black gauze. '*A whiteish light appears around her.*' Shlink's auto-obituary ('I, Wang Yen', etc.) on taking the poison is new in 1927. In 1922 the lynching party (the five characters of scene 14) propose to rape Marie, and drag her off.

16. *Shlink's Office.* (Largely rewritten as XI.)
   In 1922 John says '. . . march! Against the jungle' merely, 'of the city!' being added in 1927. Garga is off to the south to till the soil, not to New York. The play ends with a longer speech by Garga, finishing up: 'It was the best time. The chaos is used up: it dismissed me without a blessing. Maybe work will be a consolation. It's certainly very late. I feel abandoned.' Then Moti Gui's voice, off: 'East wind!' Garga remains alone, grinning.

2
In the Quarry

White chalk slope. Morning. The rumbling of the Pacific trains, off. People shouting.

George Garga. The Green Man.

GARGA *ragged, in shirt and trousers, hands in pockets:* An average morning. Anything strike you, sir?

GREEN MAN: Let's go and have another drink.

GARGA: What's that noise?

GREEN MAN: The trains to Illinois.

GARGA: Yes. As usual.

GREEN MAN: Aren't you working in a shop any longer, sir?

GARGA: It's my time off.

GREEN MAN: Let's have a drink.

GARGA: No, no.

GREEN MAN: How's the seamstress?
  Garga whistles.

GREEN MAN: Is she off too?

GARGA: The clouds! Like soiled swans! Do you enjoy having a boot put in your face?

GREEN MAN: No.

GARGA: What can one do about it?
  The Green Man pulls out a pistol.

GARGA *takes it:* We'll have a drink afterwards. It's not pleasant having a boot put in one's face.

GREEN MAN: What's he really after?

GARGA *shrugs his shoulders:* One fine morning he spat a little cherry stone in my eye.

GREEN MAN: Unknown?

GARGA: Never saw him before.

GREEN MAN: Careful. Cold blood.
  Sound of trains rumbling by above.
  That's the Pacific–New York. Will he want to dig his heels in?

GARGA: Surely.

GREEN MAN: . . . Have reckoned with you?

GARGA: I turned up out of the blue.

GREEN MAN: Having a drink is undoubtedly better. Sleeping with women. Smoking.

GARGA: Baring your teeth isn't bad.

GREEN MAN: If you've got good ones.

The Play's Literary Ancestry

A NOTE BY GERHARD NELLHAUS

At the start of the opening scene Brecht acknowledges, in the order of their importance, the two writers who particularly influenced his play. They were the Danish novelist Johannes Vilhelm Jensen (1875–1950) and the French poet Arthur Rimbaud (1854–91). In the note on pp. 72–73 he specifies the works from which, directly and indirectly, he had drawn: the novel *Hjulet* (*The Wheel*) and the prose poem *Une saison en enfer*. He knew both in the German: the former in a translation by Mens published in 1908 under the title *Das Rad*, and Rimbaud's writings in translations by K. L. Ammer (Karl Klammer) and Adolf Christian.

Of the two, the influence of *The Wheel* was the greater in every way: background and plot, characterizations, imagery, illustrations of which are given in the notes below (which are based on the German edition published by S. Fischer in 1921, since *Hjulet* has not been published in English). It is in the main the story of 'a fight between two human beings, two different types of nervous organism, a relentless fight which could only end with the extermination of one of them, because one was fighting blind and with all the strength of his basic appetite while for the other it was a question of life or death' (German edition, pp. 107–8). This was the continuation of a fight that had begun in a novel *Madam d'Ora*, which Jensen had written a year earlier, in 1904. In it the lay-preacher Evanston, a self-styled superman, destroyed the renowned scientist Edmund Hall by accusing him of his own murder of one Elly Johnson in London. But later in New York, Evanston is defeated by the young journalist, Lee, in a boxing match, 'an encounter ... which [Evanston] could not possibly forget ... [He] came to love Lee ... to long for [him], to long for [him] from the moment when [Lee] with a blow of his fist shut [Evanston's] eyes' (p. 182). Now Evanston, alias Cancer, has come to Chicago, for this was the hub of the world's wheel, 'a grand international centre ... the centre of the most materialistic philosophy in the world' (p. 165). Here Evanston starts out in a hole in the wall as a revivalist and becomes the prophet of a mass movement which he hopes to turn into a new religion. For it, Evanston wants Lee to write the new Bible because he knows

Lee's 'God is in Chicago' as well, since he has read Lee's tract proclaiming Americans as the lost people of God who in America have the opportunity of creating the vital civilization Europe might have become had the Gothic and not the Gallic influence won out.

Evanston's 'spiritual rape' of Lee consists not only of stealing the would-be poet's views of life, but of seeking to possess him physically, of alienating him from his fiancée, of charging him with a murder – just as he had done Hall – in an anonymous letter. Evanston can do this because he has studied this 'naïve young man' and knows that he is 'both a coward and full of self-importance', a 'sentimentalist' who, 'not being much for women', is 'still pure' and yet is engaged to the daughter of Chicago's richest man. A general strike organized by Cancer against the latter fails when Lee kills Evanston, this 'long extinct type who existed outside of society', in order to redeem 'his city and all his own kind'. After fleeing Chicago, first to Japan and then around the world, Lee returns to his pregnant fiancée and, learning of her father's death, quite 'sensibly' takes over the business.

By contrast, the relationship between Verlaine and Rimbaud now occupied Brecht less than it had done in *Baal*. He was more concerned with Rimbaud's literary manner, his 'concoction of words'. The Rimbaud quotations put into the mouth of Garga are often somewhat free; hence the original French is given below wherever possible for comparison. Though in Brecht's 'Statement' of 1924 (p. 67 above) he claimed also to have been quoting Verlaine, no lines comparable in style or content have been found.

1. Evanston in *The Wheel* (p. 84) says that 'it happens to be a female's pleasure to have her ears boxed by as malicious and dirty a baboon as possible'.

2. Rimbaud, *Une saison en enfer*: 'Je suis une bête, un nègre. Mais je puis être sauvé. Vous êtes de faux nègres, vous, maniaques, féroces, avares. Marchand, tu es nègre; magistrat, tu es nègre; général, tu es nègre; empereur, vieille démangeaison, tu es nègre: tu as bu d'une liqueur non taxée, de la fabrique de Satan. – Ce peuple est inspiré par la fièvre et le cancer . . . Je ne comprends pas les lois; je n'ai pas le sens moral, je suis une brute: vous vous trompez.'

3. 'Stormy the night and the sea runs high' is a line from a sentimental and trashy song 'The Sailor's Lot', for which, according to information supplied by Dr Kurt Opitz, Adolf Martel wrote

the text (about 1890) and H. W. Petrie the music (1897). It was very popular at the turn of the century, and Brecht heard it often as a child, so that it became for him the quintessence of *Kitsch*. He referred to it in *Drums in the Night*, in scene 13 of *Mahagonny*, in chapter 14 of *The Threepenny Novel* and in an unfinished essay of the 1950s on popular poetry ('Wo ich gelernt habe') where he noted that it contained 'one quatrain of great beauty'.

4. In *The Wheel* (p. 162) Lee says of Evanston, 'What was one to do about a man whose nerves hardly reached his skin?'

5. Cf. *The Wheel*, p. 221: 'In all the streets people began to move about, all the faithful early risers in the city, people like himself, whom he had always fully comprehended, whether they were driving in their waggons or were striding off with their tools, or were half-running along the sidewalk, a mountain of fresh newspapers on their shoulders.' There is a similar echo in Shen Teh's speech in scene 4 of *The Good Person of Szechwan*.

6. 'L'époux infernal' is the subheading of the first 'Délire' in *Une saison en enfer*, where the virgin exclaims, 'Je suis esclave de l'Epoux infernal, celui qui a perdu les vierges folles.'

7. Rimbaud: 'J'aimai le désert, les vergers brûlés, les boutiques fanées, les boissons tiédies.'

8. No such passage was found in Rimbaud, but perhaps Brecht was inspired by Rimbaud's lines: 'Je suis veuve ... J'étais veuve ...' in the first 'Délire' above.

9. In *The Wheel*, too, Evanston reproaches Lee for drinking.

10. 'Une souffle ouvre les brèches opératiques dans les cloisons' are the opening words of 'Nocturne Vulgaire' in *Les Illuminations*.

11. These are said to have been the dying words of Frederick the Great.

12. In *The Wheel* Lee refuses Evanston's love because he finds him so unappealing, because he 'knew instinctively that Evanston was an old man' (p. 168), 'a worm of the past' (p. 245), who fought 'with the powers of an ape and mostly with the corruption of age' (p. 297).

13. This key speech echoes both Rimbaud's 'J'enviais la félicité des bêtes' and many passages from *The Wheel*. Note Evanston's remark (p. 216) that 'the only thing real in this world is sensual lust ... the only proof I have of being alive is that I die of pleasure'. And several times Jensen describes how Evanston confronts Lee 'like a beast of prey, baring his teeth' (p. 163), and how 'they faced each other like two wild animals' (p. 280).

14. Towards the end of their fight, Lee in *The Wheel* complains of his adversary's 'endless babbling' (p. 293).

15. Rimbaud, *Une saison en enfer*: 'Je reviendrai, avec des membres de fer, la peau sombre, l'oeil furieux; sur mon masque, on me jugera d'une race forte. J'aurai de l'or: je serai oisif et brutal. Les femmes soignent ces féroces infirmes retour des pays chauds. Je serai mêlé aux affaires politiques. Sauvé.'

16. The final scene recalls what happens at the end of *The Wheel* when Lee decides to devote himself to his dead father-in-law's business: 'The everyday had returned with its chances and ways, the everyday and the old taste for work.'